GENDER AND DESTINY

Recent Titles in
Contributions in Women's Studies

MARLENE E. HEINEMANN

GENDER AND DESTINY

Women Writers and the Holocaust

CONTRIBUTIONS IN WOMEN'S STUDIES,
NUMBER 72

Greenwood Press
NEW YORK • WESTPORT, CONNECTICUT • LONDON

Library of Congress Cataloging-in-Publication Data

Heinemann, Marlene E., 1948-
  Gender and destiny.

(Contributions in women's studies, ISSN 0147–104X ;
no. 72)
  Bibliography: p.
  Includes index.
  1. Holocaust, Jewish (1939–1945)—Personal narratives
—History and criticism. 2. Holocaust, Jewish
(1939–1945), in literature. 3. Women authors. I. Title.
II. Series.
D810.J4H388 1986   940.53'15'03924   86–367
ISBN 0–313–24665–3 (lib. bdg. : alk. paper)

Library of Congress Catalog Card Number: 86–367
ISBN: 0–313–24665–3
ISSN: 0147–104X

First published in 1986

Greenwood Press, Inc.
88 Post Road West
Westport, Connecticut 06881

Printed in the United States of America

∞

The paper used in this book complies with the
Permanent Paper Standard issued by the National
Information Standards Organization (Z39.48–1984).

10 9 8 7 6 5 4 3 2 1

To my mother,
MARGOT EDITH HEINEMANN,
in recognition.

CONTENTS

ACKNOWLEDGMENTS

I am indebted to numerous people for supporting me in the completion of this project. The members of my University of Wyoming writing group deserve special recognition for hours of editing and much encouragement: especially Elizabeth Grubgeld, Gladys Crane, Jean Schaefer, and Susan Dickman. I also wish to thank the following scholars for their valuable advice and support: Henry H. H. Remak, Anne Hedin, Emil Snyder, Matei Calinescu, Alvin Rosenfeld, Joan Miriam Ringelheim, Vera Laska, Sybil Milton, the staff of the Leo Baeck Institute, Susan Pentlin and Jim Sylwester. Others who made a big difference include Bella and George Savran, Sylvia Crocker, Carrie Delgado, and Pat Walsh. I also thank the Department of Modern and Classical Languages at the University of Wyoming for the teaching position which financed the final stages of this writing, and I thank departmental secretaries Dawn Johnson and Alice Leseberg, as well as my colleague Christine Jensen, for much typing and editing assistance. Betty King also merits a warm acknowledgment for editing. I also acknowledge the American Association of University Women and the Memorial Foundation for Jewish Culture, which contributed financially to the early stages of the research for this book. Without the help of all these people and others, this book might still be fragments lying in a drawer. Its flaws, however, are entirely my responsibility.

INTRODUCTION

Why women writers of Holocaust literature? Whom have you heard of, Elie Wiesel or Livia Bitton Jackson? Primo Levi or Charlotte Delbo? Tadeusz Borowski or Gerda Klein? Even after the controversial televising of *Playing for Time*, most people I have asked have not heard of Fania Fénelon. Almost everyone knows Anne Frank, but the life of hiding which her diary describes has very little to do with the concentration camp and deaths which awaited Anne and her family, like millions of others.

Why another book on the Holocaust? Already we have more books on the systematic annihilation of two-thirds of European Jewry than any one person can master. It is not simply the singularity of the event, although that is part of the reason. Even more than the scope and violence of the destruction, it is that a modern and culturally advanced nation, significantly aided by many in other countries, used modern industrial and managerial methods to destroy a people which had "produced the inventors and communicators of that culture in disproportionate numbers."[1] Historian Henry Feingold points out the particular Jewish contribution of universalism to many fields of European intellectual thought and suggests that the Holocaust was a suicidal act of Europeans turning on those whose intellectual elite asked them to be better than they wanted to be. Although Turkey's genocide of its Armenian population in 1915 shares a number of important characteristics with the National Socialist Final Solution, the aftermath of these two events is not similar.[2] The reverberations of the Holocaust dramatically affected Europe and the rest of the world. Jewish prominence disappeared from European affairs, and some historians see this as a major cause of the postwar decline of European power and its loss of self-confidence in matters of defense.[3] Although the preconditions for the creation of Israel existed before World War II, the Holocaust intensified the need for its success while eliminating much of its potential population. It contributed to the intensity of the Arab-Israeli conflict and the key role of Israel in world affairs. The word "Auschwitz" has become a new metaphor for atrocity and evil, frequently misapplied to lesser injustices to emphasize their severity. Jews, Germans, Christians, and Arabs have a different sense of themselves in the world in the aftermath of the Holocaust. Never before in history had Christians persecuted Jews with such thoroughness. Like Gypsies, Jews became the target of hatred because they were defined as a subhuman race, and so religious conversion was not an option as it had once been in past persecutions. In the process, the National Socialists drew large numbers of others such as Slavs and political opponents into the maelstrom. Never before had humans invented such demonic methods, aided by modern technology, to debase and dehumanize victims before destroying them.

Survivors sometimes describe the death camps as beyond language because our languages were never before used to describe such a degree of organized terror. Thus the experience of surviving the Holocaust frequently means carrying memories and feelings very difficult to communicate and yet often demanding communication with those who have not been there. A leading function of Holocaust literature, then, is to allow the survivors to bear witness and to warn us about the underside of our civilization.

The study of Holocaust literature has focussed primarily on the writings of men, whose perspectives have been taken as representative of the experience of all Holocaust victims. But to assume that Holocaust literature by men represents the writings of women is to remain blind to the findings of scholarship about the significance of gender in history and literature. Men and women live in different cultural spheres in all known societies and have experienced many historical epochs and turning points in quite different ways.[4] Until examination has shown whether men and women experienced and wrote about the Holocaust in the same way, research which implies the "universality" of men's writing and experience will be inadequate.[5] Even the most impartial and sensitive male survivor will be unable to provide an insider's picture of women's experiences in the Nazi camps, since male and female prisoners were segregated in separate camps. Opportunities for observing the opposite sex in the Holocaust were greatest in the communal life of towns and ghettos; but in camps these opportunities were limited to forbidden glimpses across barbed wire fences or while marching to outdoor work sites, or to work occasionally performed by work groups in another camp. Just as one would find women's memoirs in their treatment of men's experiences to be too superficial to rely on in general, one cannot depend upon the eyewitness accounts of men to provide depth in describing the female experience. Elie Wiesel in *Night* describes only one female at Buna (a labor camp for men within the vast Auschwitz system), a girl in a warehouse where he worked who once gave him some bread and encouraged him after the foreman had attacked him.[6] In many men's memoirs and novels, glimpses of starved and ragged female inmates arouse in men an awareness of losing their protective role, or simply painful feelings, but little about the women themselves. For example, in Izaak Goldberg's memoir *The Miracles Versus Tyranny*, the sight of the sick women in Birkenau (the main extermination camp of Auschwitz) to whom this Polish Jew helps transport food convinces him never to visit the women's camp again because it depressed him more than the men's camps.[7] How could he be an eyewitness of their suffering? Or Tadeusz Borowski, who after describing several truckloads of women pleading for rescue as they are driven to the gas chambers, says, "Not one of us made a move, not one of us lifted a hand," expressing the male survivor's guilt about failing to protect, although inaction and thus possible survival was the less terrible choice in an irrational world.[8]

Analogous moments occur in women's memoirs when they

glimpse suffering male prisoners, but the women rarely refer to their loss of male protection, unless laconically. Women more often refer to the poorer physical and mental condition of the men they see and not infrequently to the efforts of the women to share their food with the men. A number of sources confirm the greater vulnerability of men than women to starvation; while both sexes perceive the other sex as more victimized, women tend to be more concrete about the greater weakness of men.[9]

Sometimes male authors incorporate specifically female experiences in their works, such as rape or prostitution, while obscuring the experience within their male perspective. For example, Borowski describes some women who went to the dentist in the Auschwitz men's camp to have their teeth pulled (probably to extract the gold, by analogy to other memoirs, but Borowski does not say). Instead they were found in sexual acts with the dentists and the orchestra conductor.

A nineteen-year-old SS man once caught the orchestra conductor, a stout respectable gentleman, and several dentists inside an ambulance in unambiguous positions with the female patients who had come to have their teeth pulled.[10]

Borowski's description hides the nature of the sexual encounter: it seems to be against the wills of the women, since they went to the dentist for another reason. The thoughts and desires of the women are omitted from the description. The author's point is merely that the incident is as ordinary as any of the other events of the camp: "An episode of this sort is no discredit to anyone: you are unlucky if you are caught, that is all."[11] He also describes the women who function as prostitutes in the Auschwitz brothel as ordinary women from whom the men seek friendship. Again the women's perspective remains unknown.

Critical scholarship about Holocaust literature that pays attention to gender issues or women writers is rare. Lawrence Langer in *Versions of Survival* and Terrence Des Pres in *The Survivor* quote from the memoirs of many women and men but do not suggest anything distinct about male and female writing or experience. There is nothing surprising about this, given the standard practice in virtually all Holocaust scholarship today.

Des Pres has given evidence of differences among men and women in death camps, but not in a published work. He wrote about it in a letter addressed to another Holocaust scholar, Joan M. Ringelheim, who did publish it. He claimed that he was "struck again and again by the ways in which, under infinitely more terrible circumstances, women in places like Auschwitz and Ravensbrück made better survivors."[12] But unfortunately his observations remained outside his widely known book. The specifics of women's experiences in the Holocaust have begun to be studied by some scholars, but the field is in its infancy.[13] The support of publishers and Holocaust historians is essential to this endeavor, and there is some evidence that it is growing.

More attention to gender issues in Holocaust literature would shed light on some unresolved disputes in the scholarship. One of these disputes is whether prisoners helped each other in significant ways. The Nazis organized the camps so that prisoners carried out on each other most of the work of torture and killing (very brutal prisoner officials could count on SS approval and hoped thus to ensure their own survival). Because the survivor documentation is contradictory about this issue, the importance of mutual assistance within the battle for survival is ambiguous. The predominance of a primarily egotistical battle for survival is usually accepted, but different commentators attribute differing importance to the evidence for help. One form of the argument against prisoner assistance is that camp life produced a hardening of the feelings in inmates, because the constant death threat and terror were too traumatic to allow normal feelings. Two well-known male survivors, Alexander Donat, author of *The Holocaust Kingdom*, and Eugen Kogon (*The Theory and Practice of Hell*), have described this phenomenon, distinguishing between help that was given and compassion which usually was not. The protection of the psyche by means of a defensive armor would seem to be an automatic mechanism, given the circumstances. Kogon, a Buchenwald political prisoner, describes both positive and negative sides to inmate "hardness": that of prisoners who, like physicians, "grew hard in order to be able to help," and of prisoners whose cruelty "ranged from repressed sexual desires all the way to sadism."[14] However, Germaine Tillion, French political prisoner at Ravensbrück, finds Kogon's remarks appropriate perhaps to men but not to women: "In the women's camps, only the most selfish in character became so hardened, while for many the incredible personal suffering only increased their concern for the needs of others."[15] Such a remark deserves some attention, not because Tillion's view can be accepted at face value, but because women's whole prior socialization as mothers and nurturers makes it likely that they responded to each other differently in the camps than did men with each other. Inmates had to modify their behavior and morality to struggle against the conditions, but some aspects of old behavior survived. Tillion's observations plead for a close comparison of prisoner relationships in men's and women's survivor literature and for taking gender into account when making generalizations about inmates in the camps and their writings.

Autobiographical and historical literature inevitably leads to questions of truth and factuality. Do we read Holocaust memoirs as historical documents? A memoir is selective personal history, conventionally more directed toward public historical events than the autobiography proper. It occupies a realm somewhere between history and imagination: the author's experience is the basis of what is said, but it is filtered through memory, feelings, and the tendency to create coherent patterns and structures. The situation of the writer in the present helps to recreate the past. When reading these memoirs, it is tempting to take what is said for fact, but safer to label what happens as theme. Many of the "themes" in memoirs seem more factual than those of novels, where everything is presumed to be fictional or typical. But the factuality of memoirs is open to question and cannot be assumed without verification from other sources. At best, Holocaust memoirs tell us what their authors remember about some of their experiences.

Besides providing memories of the Holocaust to which women have a privileged perspective, the study of women's Holocaust memoirs in the context of women's autobiographies in general can correct conclusions based on too narrow a group of texts and at the same time highlight what makes Holocaust narratives different. Patricia Meyer Spacks, in "Selves in Hiding," finds that the autobiographical act of self-revelation has been open to few women until recently, and the majority of female autobiographers have had careers as artistic performers, with "their demand for public attention in modes relatively acceptable for women predating their written self-description." While one may agree that "the housewife seldom offers her life to public view," the person who surveys the available memoirs will conclude that an artistic career is not a prerequisite for women writing about the Holocaust.[16] Gerda Klein is a speaker for Jewish organizations, Livia Jackson is a professor of Judaica, and Judith Dribben is a translator besides her career in the Israeli army. One of the unique characteristics of this literature is that ordinary people leading ordinary lives were hurled into a cataclysm which called forth in them exceptional actions, and if they survived, often the impulse to write about their experience.

Another statement which needs qualification is that of Estelle Jelinek, who finds that women's autobiographies avoid referring to political and historical events, even when the authors have had political or other careers.[17] Women's Holocaust memoirs, defined by a historical period, necessarily show women confronting the particulars of that event. However, women often emphasize personal relationships more than do men within the same context.

While it seems that no one has counted the available memoirs, a fairly large number of Holocaust texts have been written by women. Sidra Ezrahi has noticed that women have written a high percentage of what she calls survival novels and compares her impressions to those of Robert Lifton, who noticed a surprisingly high number of female writers of Japanese A-bomb literature.[18] If the will to bear witness to extreme collective suffering is the predominant motive for writing such documents, it would make sense that women would feel keenly this responsibility to the dead and the living and that this feeling of responsibility would overcome personal and cultural inhibitions against self-display in an autobiographical work. The conditioning of females to take the needs of others more seriously than their own needs is powerful enough to explain why they have written a relatively large number of personal narratives.

Description of Method

The guiding aim of this book is to explore ways to describe Holocaust narratives from the perspective of gender, especially that of women. Most of the analysis is based on five memoirs and one novel by women authors. Three memoirs by men also serve for a discussion involving lengthy gender comparisons, and several other memoirs and novels have been cited as needed. The territory is charted according to a four-part plan: first, a thematic study of some experiences specific to females in the Nazi camps; second, an examination of varieties of characterization in the texts; third, a comparison of male and female inmate relations in selected texts; and fourth, a consideration of factors contributing to credibility and authenticity in these Holocaust texts. The first and third chapters are occupied with the delineation of a gender-specific experience in the concentration camps. The second and fourth chapters, on characterization and authenticity, respectively, treat general Holocaust literature issues (non-gender specific) through the six chosen women's texts. The chapter on characterization demonstrates that Holocaust narratives exhibit a variety of survivor characters despite some similarity of experiences from one text to another, and I have included some speculation about possible reasons. The variety of character types also contradicts a theory of women's autobiographical self-portraits. The chapter on authenticating strategies is a way of addressing the rather different claims to veracity which the reader experiences in reading different texts.

The decision to analyze both fictional and autobiographical texts was made in the interest of extending the range of the research and to develop a model of characterization which would encompass both novels and memoirs. Although important differences exist in the use of time and the expectations of truth in fiction and memoirs, the particular focus in this study on literary aspects of both genres seemed to allow treating them together. As several critics have commented, the dividing line between fiction and non-fiction is exceptionally difficult to draw in Holocaust literature, as many memoirs have been embellished with fictional elements, and novels have often been structured as imitation memoirs. It is easier to separate diaries from other narrative forms, since the time of narration is closer to being immediately after the event so that memory lapses are less significant. In *A Double Dying*, Alvin Rosenfeld includes diaries and memoirs in his chapter "Holocaust and History," but he discusses Leon Wells' *The Janowska Road*, a fictionalized memoir, in "Imagination in Extremis" along with Tadeusz Borowski's *This Way for the Gas, Ladies and Gentlemen*.[19] These two accounts are by survivors, employ fictional techniques, and contest previous fictional conventions. It is not entirely clear what distinguishes memoir from fiction, because intermediate forms defy strict definition. When memoirs rely on a detached objectivity, they are conventionally assigned to non-fiction. However, many Holocaust memoirs use a combination of fictional and non-fictional elements. To simplify these problems, the difference between memoir and novel is considered here to be one of conventional claims to truth: the reader believes that the memoir refers to events actually experienced by the author, while taking the historical novel to represent imagined but typical events. But for much of the discussion, all the texts can be treated as literary texts, which convey real or typical events through a combination of memory and imagination. These issues will be discussed further in Chapter 4.

The choice of texts was determined by several criteria which needed to be balanced together. A desire to have representations from each of the three languages known to me, namely English, French, and German, was one determinant. This meant the exclusion of a great many languages, but this limitation was mitigated by the fact that many Holocaust survivors are European immigrants who write in English or other widely known languages. Two of the three texts originally written in English were written by survivors of Polish origin. The selection was also affected by an interest in the Jewish experience of the Holocaust, since conditions were generally far worse for Jews, and anti-semitism was central to the theory and practice of the Holocaust.[20] Five of the texts have Jewish or part-Jewish authors, and Charlotte Delbo, a non-Jew, incorporates the Jewish experience into the fabric of her memoir. Several non-Jewish German writers were relegated to peripheral comments, although they have written eloquently about concentration camps, because their camp status was so much higher than that of the others as to be only marginally comparable. The perspective of spiritual resistance is represented here by Livia Bitton Jackson's *Elli*, a memoir by a Hungarian survivor which somewhat resembles but is superior to Ilse Aichinger's *Herod's Children*. Superior quality was the chief factor in selecting Charlotte Delbo and Susan Fromberg Schaeffer. The insights of a female perspective of the Holocaust made a strong case for Charlotte Delbo, Fania Fénelon, Judith Dribben, and novelist Susan Fromberg Schaeffer. The need for a variety of experiences also led to the choice of Judith Dribben as partisan and Gerda Klein as traditional, religious Polish Jew. References have also been made to a number of German-speaking authors, including Ella Lingens-Reiner, Judith Sternberg Newman, Ilse Aichinger, and Jenny Spritzer.

Some attention had to be paid to providing analogous situations for comparison as well as providing variety. The fact that Delbo, Fénelon, and Dribben all write about experiences in Birkenau, a death camp, was felt to be an authenticating factor, even though prisoner status varied a good deal. Similarly, the unifying factor of the labor camp experience in Klein's memoir and Schaeffer's novel could provide a guarantee of comparability.

The texts selected for examination were all written after the end of World War II, but their dates of publication span a period of twenty-three years. The titles and their dates of publication are as follows: Gerda Klein, *All But My Life*, 1957; Charlotte Delbo, *None of Us Will Return*, 1965; Judith Dribben, *A Girl Called Judith Strick*, 1970; Susan Fromberg Schaeffer, *Anya*, 1974; Fania Fénelon, *Playing for Time*, 1976; and Livia Bitton Jackson, *Elli*, 1980. If one asks when these books were written, one of the dates can be moved back to 1945: Charlotte Delbo wrote her memoir twenty years before publishing it.[21] Whether an author, especially a survivor, chooses to write a memoir or novel immediately after the war or thirty years later would seem to make some difference in perspective and attention to detail. To what extent the date of publication of the six texts selected signals internal differences will be considered in Chapters 2 and 4.

This is not a basic reference work on the concentration camps, but wherever possible, definitions and brief explanations of camp phenomena have been included in the text. There are[*] many good books which provide a general background to the Holocaust and more complete descriptions of the camps.[22]

Notes

1. Henry L. Feingold, "Determining the Uniqueness of the Holocaust: The Factor of Historical Valence," *Shoah* 2, no. 2 (Spring, 1981): 10.

2. Helen Fein, *Accounting for Genocide* (New York: The Free Press, 1979), pp. 4–6, 10–18, 29–30.

3. Feingold, p. 6; William Pfaff, "Reflections (Finlandization)," *The New Yorker* (September 1, 1980): 31.

4. Joan Kelly (Gadol), "The Social Relations of the Sexes: Methodological Implications of Women's History," *Signs* 1, no. 4 (Summer, 1976): 812.

5. Joan Miriam Ringelheim, "The Unethical and the Unspeakable: Women and the Holocaust," *Simon Wiesenthal Center Annual* 1 (1984), pp. 69–70.

6. Elie Wiesel, *Night; Dawn; The accident; Three tales* (New York: Hill and Wang, 1972), pp. 60–61.

7. Izaak Goldberg, *The Miracles Versus Tyranny* (New York: Philosophical Library, 1978), p. 326.

8. Tadeusz Borowski, *This Way for the Gas, Ladies and Gentlemen*, trans. Barbara Veader (New York: Penguin, 1980), p. 116.

9. Ino Arndt, "Das Frauenkonzentrationslager Ravensbruck," in *Studien zur Geschichte der Konzentrationslager* (Stuttgart: Deutsche Verlags-Anstalt, 1970), pp. 120–21; and Hanna Lévy-Hass, *Inside Belsen*, trans. Ronald Taylor (Great Britain and New Jersey: The Harvester Press and Barnes and Noble, 1982), pp. 5–7.

10. Borowski, pp. 108–9.

11. Ibid., p. 109.

12. Ringelheim, p. 72.

13. See Renate Bridenthal, Atina Grossmann, Marion Kaplan, eds., *When Biology Became Destiny: Women in Weimar and Nazi Germany* (New York: Monthly Review Press, 1984); Esther Katz and Joan Miriam Ringelheim, eds., *Proceedings of the Conference Women Surviving the Holocaust* (New York: Institute for Research in History, 1983); Vera Laska, ed., *Women in the Resistance and in the Holocaust: The Voices of Eyewitnesses* (Westport, Conn.: Greenwood Press, 1983); and Joan Miriam Ringelheim, "The Unethical and the Unspeakable: Women and the Holocaust," *Simon Wiesenthal Center Annual* 1 (1984), pp. 69–87.

14. Eugen Kogon, *The Theory and Practice of Hell* (New York: Octagon-Farrar, Straus and Giroux, 1973), p. 277.

15. Germaine Tillion, *Ravensbrück* (Garden City, N.Y.: Doubleday, 1975), p. 230.

16. Patricia Meyer Spacks, "Selves in Hiding," in Estelle C. Jelinek, *Women's Autobiography: Essays in Criticism* (Bloomington: Indiana University Press, 1980), p. 112.

17. Jelinek, p. 10.

18. Robert J. Lifton, *Death in Life: Survivors of Hiroshima* (New York: Vintage, 1967), p. 474.

19. Alvin H. Rosenfeld, *A Double Dying* (Bloomington: Indiana University Press, 1980), pp. 40–61, 63–65.

20. Against standard practice, I have used the lowercase for anti-semitism to signal the word's inadequacy. Modern Semitic peoples include Arabs, but they are never meant when anti-Semitism is used. At least anti-semitism is a step removed from the Semites.

21. See Ringelheim, "The Unethical and the Unspeakable," p. 83, n. 4 (conversation of April, 1980). Also quoted in Rosette C. Lamont, "Literature, the Exile's Agent of Survival: Alexander Solzhenitsyn and Charlotte Delbo," *Mosaic* 9, no. 1 (Fall, 1975): 11.

22. See Alex Grobman and Daniel Landes, eds., *Genocide* (Los Angeles: The Simon Wiesenthal Center, and Chappaqua, N.Y.: Rossel Books, 1983); Terrence Des Pres, *The Survivor: An Anatomy of Life in the Death Camps* (New York: Oxford University Press, 1976); Lucy S. Dawidowicz, *The War Against the Jews 1933–1945* (New York: Bantam, 1976); Raul Hilberg, *The Destruction of the European Jews* (New York: Holmes and Meier, 1985, rev. ed.) or (Chicago: Quadrangle Books, Inc., 1961).

I

FEMALE-CENTERED THEMES:
ANATOMY AND DESTINY

Many writers of the Holocaust, both survivors and non-survivors, deny the significance of a specifically female experience of the Holocaust. No one articulates the overall view of universal vulnerability better than Mary Ellman, author of *Thinking About Women*, who sees in the mass annihilations of World War II the death blow to the traditional concept of sex roles.

In the atomic bombing of Hiroshima and Nagasaki, and in the murder of six million Jewish men, women and children in Europe, in the same manner and for the same cause, without distinctions in age, sex or responsibility (all were equally responsible for being alive and human), the modern concept of mutual vulnerability was established, before which the traditional sexual contrasts of strength and weakness, courage and timidity, authority and subservience became meaningless.[1]

The Nazis' intention and the Jews' and Gypsies' overriding experience is mass genocide. Other writers come to essentially the same conclusion in discussing the treatment of all inmates in the camps. Anna Pawełczyńska, a Polish survivor and sociologist, says that all former sexual distinctions based upon social and biological roles, the division of labor, and forms of respect were eliminated: "traces of these distinctions were only reflected in extra possibilities for tormenting and humiliating prisoners."[2]

She does not elaborate on the "extra possibilities." Cynthia Haft's *The Theme of Nazi Concentration Camps in French Literature* supports the belief in equal treatment when she states that the valued ability to endure pain silently is "found in women and men equally because the camp system grants complete equality to men and women."[3] This assertion of an equality of experience betrays an aspect which is not equal and which these writers choose to ignore: stoicism is generally socialized in males more than females or associated with the male role. Is the level of suffering so high that precamp experience has no relevance?

If the focus of study is the individual's chances for survival, some writers have asserted that prewar experiences did have a noticeable effect. Pawełczyńska's *Values and Violence in Auschwitz* notes that a tolerance to cold favored survival chances, while being accustomed to comfort did not. Training in practical trades or medicine also increased survival chances. This would not favor homebound women from warmer climates.[4] On the other hand, historian Raul Hilberg noticed that men did not survive as well the loss of children and family members as women who lost their families.[5] Some scholars who have described women active in organized Resistance activities have noted that sometimes they could pass more easily as non-Jews than men for both anatomical and cultural reasons. Unlike men, they were not marked by circumcision, and the Nazis did not so often suspect a woman to be engaged in secret activities against them.[6]

To determine whether gender makes an important difference in the experience of the Holocaust, an obvious area to examine is the biological roles by which patriarchal society has generally defined women: fertility and sexuality. The female body has been the chief cultural locus of both these human biological functions. The predominant role of women as parents and as cultural symbols of human sexuality like Eve suggest the importance of the female as body in Western culture. A cursory glance at the roles of women in Judaism and Christianity confirms these patterns.

Nazi policy toward women in the ghettos and camps focuses attention on these biological roles. Especially for mothers deported with children under fifteen, "gender is destiny," as historian Gerald Reitlinger points out:

Throughout the twenty-eight months of selections at Auschwitz . . .
children under fifteen, men over fifty, and women over forty-five went
to the gas chambers. To save the SS difficulties all mothers who accompanied young children went to the gas chambers, irrespective of
their age.[7]

The women and girls who were permitted to enter the camps
were exploited as slave laborers in conditions comparable to
those of the male deportees. However, women whose pregnancy showed up after admission to the camps were usually put
to death, or labor was induced early and the infant killed.[8] Sometimes pregnancy in the camps became the pretext for additional
tortures, beatings, and/or a live death in the crematory ovens.[9]
Some expectant mothers at Auschwitz were able to save their
own lives by having secret abortions with the help of some
inmate physicians or killing their babies.[10] At certain periods in
other camps, small children were allowed to live, but they usually succumbed to disease and starvation within a few months.[11]
A few were hidden and survived.

Sexuality was an extra source of vulnerability or extra food for
females in towns, ghettos, and camps. While historians have
traditionally dispensed with this subject with a reference to the
prisoners' lack of interest in sex because of starvation and the
Nazis' prohibition of sex between "Aryans" and Jews, the facts
as presented in oral and written testimony focus on the close
relationship among sex, domination, and food. The raping of
Jewish women was forbidden for the same reason as intermar-
riage. It was considered *Rassenschande*, race defilement, a con-
tamination of "Aryan" blood. "The Law for the Protection of
German blood and German Honor" of September 15, 1935,
promised imprisonment, hard labor, or transfer to the war front
for sexual relations between Jews and "Aryans." However, evidence suggests that rape did occur, perhaps due to the delay or
irregularity of punishment, primarily in various ghettos,[12] during *Kristallnacht*,[13] and in first-phase violence of the *Einsatzgrup-
pen* (mobile killing units) in Russia and Eastern Europe.[14] The
following testimony, by Gertrude Schneider, a Czech survivor
of the Riga ghetto in Poland, represents the statements of many

other survivors. A participant of a 1983 conference of women survivors, she responded to the following question:

Participant 1: Did women play up to the guards sexually?
Gertrude Schneider: They didn't have to; the guards raped you. To play up is to gain time or food. In this case, the guards were outside the ghetto and walked around; they found ways to get into the ghetto and in the night looted and raped. It was felt by the German Jews that the best way to fight this, since there was no other way, was to go to the German commandant and tell him. And Krauser made an end of it. He sent three of the Latvian SS to the front and the others stopped.[15]

This and other testimony reveals that rape did occur in ghettos and even some camps despite subsequent punishment. Furthermore, this survivor reveals a few sentences later that Krauser, a commandant, was himself above the law and protected from punishment for *Rassenschande*. He apparently made use of this protection.

While rape seems to have affected only a small minority of women in concentration camps, other forms of sexual control and abuse were more frequent. The presence of prostitution among prisoners in ghettos and camps to varying degrees is simply evidence of the overwhelming reality of starvation for most prisoners and the existence of privileged prisoner functionaries as well as the SS, who could provide extra bread for sex. While the SS set up brothels in some camps staffed by female prisoners, these affected only a small number of inmates. However, many survivors have testified to the commonness of prostitution in ghettos and camps. For example, German Jewish survivor Ruth Alton, describing the Lodz ghetto: "Only the fewest were content with one woman only. Love was very cheap. Many sold themselves for a little soup."[16] The choices presented to prisoners were extremely difficult, and in the context of starvation and death, women found that traditional dignity had to be sacrificed.

The most universal form of sexual assault on women appears to have been verbal abuse, especially immediately upon entrance to a concentration camp. Sexual verbal humiliation was an effective way of quickly demonstrating the utter powerlessness of the new female inmates. According to Vera Laska, the verbal and often physical abuse "was one of the cruelest tortures to which women were subjected in the concentration camps. . . . To many women it meant an unforgivable and never to be forgotten humiliation."[17] Because prostitution, verbal and physical sexual abuse, and at times rape were experiences special to women in the Holocaust, in addition to the especially high mortality of pregnant women and mothers, it is obvious that those who deny a gender-specific Holocaust experience have not looked at the facts. Indeed the history of gender distinctions in the Holocaust is only now beginning to be written.

The different maternal and sexual roles of women are obvious areas of divergence from male experience, whatever the social context. It is possible to see echoes and perhaps even causes of the differential treatment if Nazi policies to women in general and Jews are considered. While mothers of "inferior races" (Jews, Gypsies, and Poles) were useless as slave labor and thus gassed quickly, the maternal role for other women was idealized and encouraged through extensive legislation to increase the German birth rate. Women were excluded from higher level positions and the professions, discouraged from higher education, and hired as low-paid labor when needed by the German war machine. Women and men were expected to sacrifice their personal desires to the good of the state, but women were more severely limited. Some writers have seen considerable sexual repression connected with the fascist version of "chaste maternity."[18]

The sexual side of the Nazi treatment of women has a telling prologue in Hitler's *Mein Kampf*. Here he defines the Jew as the poison or polluter infecting the blood of the master race. Corrupt sexuality in the form of prostitution is one of Hitler's obsessions, an activity which he associates with outbreaks of syphilis. He attaches such importance to combatting this disease that he says it "should have been made to appear as *the* task of the nation."[19] He indicts the Jewish male as the force behind prostitution while virtually ignoring the role of the Jewish woman. "When thus for the first time I recognized the Jew as the cold-hearted, shameless, and calculating director of this revolting vice traffic in the scum of the big city, a cold shudder ran down my back."[20] Hitler blames Jewish men not only for prostitution, but also for rape and white slave traffic, thus allowing him to claim the need to protect pure ("Aryan") womanhood from Jewish sexual vice.

With satanic joy in his face the black-haired Jewish youth lurks in wait for the unsuspecting girl whom he defiles with his blood, thus stealing her from her people. With every means he tries to destroy the racial foundations of the people he has set out to subjugate.[21]

Hitler rarely refers to Jewish women separately, perhaps because they do not figure in his imagery of blond-haired German females at the mercy of the sexual evil of Jewish males. Nevertheless, in Holocaust literature it is usually women who receive the designation of sexual impurity from Nazi officials.

It was the fate of all Jews (except for a few survivors) to be killed quickly or slowly, i.e., to be gassed on arrival or to be first exploited as slave labor, but Jewish women were damned twice: first, maternity consigned deported women with a child under the age of fifteen to death without the reprieve of labor. Paternity did not directly affect the survival chances of Jewish males. Second, the designation of sexual impurity made the Jewish woman vulnerable to sexual exploitation and abuse which at times presented her with a choice between death and survival through prostitution. Sexual abuse and ordinary camp labor were two intertwined aspects of the female deportees' experience.

These experiences specific to women in the Holocaust will be discussed as themes in the literature which forms the object of this study, with some reference to other sources. Preceding the thematics of motherhood will be a discussion of menstruation and amenorrhea, since the two subjects are related aspects of the assault on fertility. Following these sections is a study of the theme of sexual abuse.

Menstruation and Amenorrhea

"It's upsetting not to go through those unclean periods," Hilde reflected. "You begin to feel like an old woman." Timidly, Big Irene asked: "And what if they never come back afterwards?" At her words a ripple of horror swept over us. . . . Catholics crossed themselves, others recited the Shema; everyone tried to exorcise this curse the Germans were holding over us: sterility. How could one sleep after that?"[22]

The conditions of ghettos and concentration camps affected nearly all females above the age of puberty with the threat of infertility. While mothers of younger children and most pregnant women were immediately killed and forced sterilization was practiced on some women and men, the phenomenon of amenorrhea is at once less severe and more universal among all but the most privileged inmates. Some writers attribute the lapse of menstruation to the poor food or trauma, others to a drug put in the soup, but it is nearly always mentioned in the memoirs of women. Amenorrhea must be considered a form of psychological assault on a woman's identity, since most women had no idea whether fertility would return if they survived. It threatened them with the loss of the specific biological function which society insists upon as the chief vocation for women. Thus the loss of fertility could be construed as a threat to the possibility of a worthwhile life "afterwards." Two commonly treated aspects of the theme of menstruation are the fear of infertility and the awkwardness or danger of menstruation in extremity. In Holocaust fiction such as *Anya* one finds the regenerative symbolism of returning or persistent bleeding.

The fear of permanent infertility is treated in *Playing for Time* by Fénelon and *All But My Life* by Gerda Klein. In Fénelon, the fear is collective, linking the privileged orchestra girls with ordinary inmates while separating them from an anonymous and envied culprit who leaves a pile of used napkins in a double bass case. Fénelon expresses the collective question that haunted the orchestra women, who had an above-average chance to survive: would survival come at the cost of their fertility? It is worth noting that even a professional singer who expresses no interest in future marriage equates femininity with fertility. In contrast, Gerda Klein's personal fear of infertility seems to divide her from the indifference, perhaps feigned, of the others. It fuels her daydreams of maternity after liberation. Her romantic relationship with Kurt Klein after liberation implies rather than reveals the return of fertility. Their relationship begins when he, as a liberating soldier, asks her whether she and her comrades were sterilized, and she replies that they were not.[23]

The curse of infertility is nearly matched by the awkwardness of continued menstrual periods in camps, where even rags and water were usually lacking. Unstopped bleeding became an additional reason for beatings from block leaders.[24] Livia Jackson, barely old enough to menstruate, communicates her horror at seeing blood flowing freely down the legs of a girl at roll call, "I would rather die than have blood flowing down my legs." Her ingenuous reaction conveys some of the surreality of the camp: "Does menstruating constitute sabotage?"[25] The continued menstrual periods of the heroine of *Anya* signify both increased vulnerability and biological resistance against the Nazi assault on Jewish maternity. While Anya is resting because of cramps from her privileged job as maid in Kaiserwald, soldiers try to rape her, and her escape to Riga is complicated by a sudden heavy flow requiring a risky stop in an apothecary shop for rest and a calcium injection. But Anya's awkward bleeding after her escape also serves as a concrete symbol of her strength and vitality, her capacity to endure with fertility intact. In this way, the novel resembles *Tell Me Another Morning* by Zdena Berger, where the onset of menstruation signals a renewal of the life forces for the survivor.[26] However, the epilogue of *Anya* undercuts this optimism by showing the middle-aged survivor's worries about feeling sterile.

Amenorrhea is important as a nearly universal female experience in the concentration and death camps. It suggests that the fear of infertility was much more widespread than the actual incidence of the more extreme forced sterilization. Of the six texts studied, only in Delbo does fear become reality: this author devotes one episode to the sterilization of men; the event is not dramatized but instead reflected in the faces of prisoners waiting in line outside the women's infirmary. The sterilization of women is consigned to a brief statement at the end of the episode. The quicker process of male sterilization allows the author to describe the confrontation of the men waiting and those leaving the infirmary, a confrontation between resignation and humiliation:

"They put their clothes back on at the threshold. Their eyes avoid those of the others who wait. And when we can see their faces we understand. How could we describe the distress in their gestures? The humiliation in their eyes?"[27]

The assault on male fertility also suggests an assault on male sexuality, a theme otherwise lacking in the memoir.

In view of the nearly universal fear of sterility associated with camp amenorrhea and the positive attitude toward the return of the menses in the survivor, the view of menstruation in Holocaust literature runs counter to longstanding cultural attitudes which condemn menstruation. The taboos in Judaism surrounding menstruating women have been traced to a male castration anxiety originating in primitive tribes but apparently still present today.[28] In the present century, "the most influential psychoanalytic literature concerning menstruation continues to view this common and at times bothersome process as a 'monthly neurosis' fraught with fears of castration, maternal revenge, anal repulsion, and lost children."[29] In the literature surveyed here, the loss of menstruation signals the functional castration of targeted women by the Nazi system, and its return in the survivor promises the return of life and the possibility of a future. As such it goes against the grain of the official attitudes often attributed to this function.

Maternity and Childbirth

I can feel it in my body how it did happen. Every muscle in her is beating out the birth and yet she wants to hold back, to stop up the bowels of birth because she knows... what did that woman say?... The baby was bitten the moment it was born by the spotted-fever lice....

There but for the grace of God and there is no grace of God, we see that there is none—so I go side-slipping into the life of that woman who gave birth in the typhus-infested straw. Sometimes I feel I am her more than I am myself. I feel myself moving toward her image the way the weaker field of vision in a stereopticon gets drawn to the stronger.[30]

Since motherhood made women a target population in the death camps and sometimes the ghettos, it is not surprising that mothers and children figure prominently in many Holocaust texts by women. Some of the aspects of the theme of maternity and survival which are highlighted in the literature and will be discussed here are young mothers targeted for extermination, the separation between mothers and daughters, efforts to overcome separation, an SS woman tempted by the maternal role, and the theme of childbirth in the camps.

Three categories of mothers had very low chances of survival. Mothers arrested with small children, mothers and women above age forty-five, and women who gave birth in the camps were usually gassed immediately. *Anya* and *None of Us Will Return* are two works which show the fate of young mothers who must lead their children to annihilation. In *Anya*, mothers have to give their children to the Nazis in the ghetto or be attacked by their dogs. At the selection point between the ghetto and the trains, Nazis ferret out hiding mothers by using their small children like bird dogs to point out their mothers. Anya has hidden her daughter Ninka just in time with Christians. The impossibility of moral choice in this situation is reflected in the opposite reactions of Anya and her mother: Anya's frightened realization that very little has separated her from the fate of these wretched mothers, while her mother exonerates a mother who is hiding to survive:

"No," I kept shaking my head; "no." I had come so close; Ninka had come so close. One woman in our line was crouched down in back of us. "She must have left a child," Momma whispered after it was over; "see how she hid herself? So she is saved, and this is how it is."[31]

Years later, in her epilogue, Anya wonders how these women could go on living after leaving their children: what purpose can life have for them? Her mother, spared this dilemma through her age and early death, has the detachment from the events to affirm life for its own sake. The mother alone may survive, while the child alone could not.[32]

In Delbo's *None of Us Will Return*, the narrator is an inmate observing mothers and children among the procession of new arrivals heading for the gas chambers. The narrator observes a mother disciplining her child with futile gestures which arouse futile emotions in the observers: "She slaps her child and we who know do not forgive her for it. Besides it would make no difference if she were to smother him with kisses."[33] Delbo does not particularly distinguish the death of mothers and children from the mass annihilation described in the first episode of the work. However, this scene is the first instance of a well-developed theme of the loss of mothers and maternal care.

The most frequent treatment of the maternity theme in the literature is that of the separation between mother and daughter. The protagonist in many memoirs and novels is a teenaged daughter or young adult who survives after separation from her family. A typical moment in Holocaust literature is the climactic moment of separation from the family. The segregation of the sexes ensures that the last relative from whom a girl separates will be her mother or another woman. In Schaeffer, Delbo, Klein, Dribben, and Fénelon, daughters separate forever from mothers too old to enter the camps or too weak or unlucky to survive them. In Klein the moment of separation is silent, but in many cases the mother shouts something to her daughter, a last verbal inheritance to encourage her to live, often to prevent her from trying to die with her. "You will live! You have someone for whom to live!" Rebecca Savikin shouts to her daughter Anya after selection, in which the old, weak, or sick are separated out and sent away to be killed. While trying to run to safety in a camp, a mother in Delbo is caught and selected for death. She says to her daughter, "Get away. Run. Leave me."[34] The mothers ask to be abandoned so that their daughters can try to survive.

Mothers and daughters sometimes transcend their separation in the works by struggling to remain together, through a later reunion, or symbolically through memory or friendship. In Jackson's *Elli* the young narrator succeeds in overcoming separations wrought by her mother's illness and other events by disobeying SS rules and thus risking her own death; driven by need, she is saved by luck as well as initiative. In *Anya*, the heroine hides her daughter with Christians before the selections against children and mothers and finds her again after escaping from a labor camp and hiding in other places; their almost miraculous reunion is qualified by their estrangement in the present time of narration. In Delbo, the lost mother returns symbolically as an image of unexpected strength in moments of greatest suffering. Standing at roll call during a freezing winter night, the narrator says, "I see my mother with the mask of resolute will that her face has become. My mother. Far away. I do not look at anything. I do not think anything."[35] The maternal image objectifies strength and will in a landscape so extreme that consciousness and vision shrink to the bare essentials. In two other moments of extremity, friends help the narrator and become associated with her mother's strength. Moments after the vision cited above, when the narrator falls unconscious to the icy ground, her friend Viva brings her back from the sweet temptation of death:

She calls and calls my name which comes to me from far away from unfathomable emptiness—it is the voice of my mother that I hear. The voice grows hard: "Heads up. On your feet." And I feel that I cling to Viva as much as a child clings to its mother. I cling to the woman who has kept me from falling into the slush, into the snow from which one does not get up again.[36]

The maternal memory image establishes the dependent relationship between the narrator and Viva at a moment when the greater strength of the latter seems immense to the weaker one, as great as the strength of a mother to a helpless infant. The strong voice allows her to return to the terrible adult struggle which is consciousness in these conditions.

Other works also communicate the symbolic transcendence of the loss of mothers and family through memory. Such memories mentally resurrect a secure past and thus an aspect of the deportee's former self temporarily, thus challenging the total power of extremity over consciousness.[37] In some works, memory acts as self-delusion at least temporarily. In Klein, the survivor continues to daydream intermittently about family reunions after liberation long after her rational mind knows that her parents and brother have died. This delusion is clearly a survival strategy because it gives Klein a reason to endure.

Holocaust memoirs and novels, such as those by Schaeffer and Klein, emphasize hiding family photographs to protect them from seizure as another way to reinforce memory. Anya retains memories of her mother, like other family members and friends, in the form of proverbial quotations and survival lessons. As panic spreads in the boxcar during her deportation to Kaiserwald, she hears her mother's voice: "They are all going crazy now, Anya; you don't have to go with them."[38] Still more common are her recurrent memories of her mother, repeating words of traditional feminine wisdom: "A woman has to look her best," Momma was saying as I took out my mirror, and then: "You will survive; you have for whom to survive."[39] These two lessons are key guideposts for Anya's survival actions in the novel. She rationalizes the emotional trauma of loss, formulating family memories as proverbs guiding action. However, in the post-Holocaust section, memory entraps the survivor in the past, preventing her from living fully in the present.

The motherhood of many targeted women as portrayed in the narratives usually created additional suffering and vulnerability for them. The problem of maternity in the Holocaust world finds another expression when the focus is one of the female torturers. While many memoirs comment on the coexistence of beauty and cruelty in the SS women, few of them have treated the pairing of maternal feelings and cruelty. Fania Fénelon provides a glimpse of this from her privileged view of Maria Mandel, SS Lagerführerin of Birkenau. This SS woman temporarily saves a Polish child destined for the ovens, "a ringleted angel of two or three," leaving its mother and thousands of Polish "Aryan" women to their doom. She marches "among . . . those crouching women as one would walk through a snake pit: furious and disgusted."[40] Mandel drops her cold military role and plays mother to this child for a week, showing him off to deportees in Birkenau. At the end of the week, she takes the toddler to the gas chamber herself to follow the already cremated Poles. Fénelon presents the Nazi's behavior as a role conflict between maternal feelings and her duty to follow orders. The portrait of the SS officer apparently touched by a deported child is a good example of humanity coupled with barbarism in one of the executioners. Only after the child has been killed do her eyes betray suffering when she comes to the orchestra, asking Fénelon to sing her favorite aria from *Madame Butterfly* and leaving without a sign.

Sidra Ezrahi's analysis of the predominantly female-authored genre she calls "survival fiction" includes childbirth in the camps as one of its recurrent themes. Ezrahi limits her discussion to novels, especially Ilona Karmel's *An Estate of Memory*; however, her emphasis on the thematic importance of childbirth also applies to many Holocaust memoirs.[41] Since childbirth in ghettos was difficult and, in camps, punishable by death, the event was often an unhappy occasion. Sometimes the mother could save her own life by killing or having another person kill her newborn infant. A writer like Judith Sternberg Newman reacts only with horror and disapproval, but Olga Lengyel describes the more finely shaded morality which justifies the actions for her:

And so the Germans succeeded in making murderers of even us. To this day the picture of those murdered babies haunts me. . . . The only meager consolation is that by these murders we saved the mothers. Without our intervention, they would have endured worse sufferings, for they would have been thrown into the crematory ovens while still alive.[42]

The camp childbirth theme finds a more positive treatment when newborn infants are successfully hidden from the SS. Usually the survival of a baby provides a powerful signal of the life force to women inmates. In Reska Weiss' *Journey Through Hell*, women inmates of Neumark treat a newborn infant as their common possession and draw from the sight of it the strengthening memory of their own children at home.[43] A scene of childbirth in Fania Fénelon's memoir conveys the intense drama and impact of childbirth on the narrator in the chaotic conditions of Bergen-Belsen, which surpassed even Auschwitz in horror near the end of the war. Fania helps her friend Marie, a physician, to deliver a Polish woman of her baby in the Bergen-Belsen infirmary. The incident illustrates resistance action which is at once life-affirming, heroic, and suggestive of a latent survival wisdom in the narrator. She discovers that her hands know what to do even though she has never performed these actions before and that they have an extraordinary power to revitalize: "I forgot the immense weariness that was making me so indifferent, which cut me off from the effort of living. I was super-alive, super-excited, and I wanted to shout: 'That's it, he's born.' "[44] Thus the three women cheat the Nazis of two lives by hiding the mother and child in the infirmary until liberation, which occurs soon afterward. Fénelon's excitement over new and unforeseen life in the chaos, starvation, and filth of Bergen-Belsen suggests the upbeat rhythm of resistance and a heroism of lifesaving specific to women's experience in the camps.

Sexual Abuse

A couple of months previous (Tauber) had brought a thousand women out into the snow, lined them up, entirely naked, in the freezing air, then, moving along their ranks, lifted their breasts with the tip of his whip. Those whose breasts sagged went to the left, those whose breasts remained firm went to the right and were spared a little longer, except of course for those who perished from the cold.[45]

The theme of sexual violence and humiliation recurs in many of the Holocaust works written by and about women. While the exchange of sex for greater survival odds may at times be part of the male prisoners' experience, it occurs only in more restricted forms in the male-written literature surveyed. Usually it is voluntary and involves a homosexual relationship between a younger person, "the pipel," and a *kapo*, i.e., a prisoner functionary. Heterosexual relations occurred sometimes between male skilled workers and female *kapos* in a women's camp.[46] However, the exploitation of sexual abuse by SS officials as an instrument of terror and control occurs primarily between SS officials, either male or female, and the female inmates. Only in women's camps were those in power of both sexes. In men's camps, SS and functionary positions were always filled by men.

Some male writers have treated sexual victimization in the Holocaust, almost invariably of women. Both Tadeusz Borowski and Ka-Tzetnik 135633 treat the phenomenon of the prisoner brothel at Auschwitz reserved for the use of the SS and prisoner elite. In *This Way for the Gas, Ladies and Gentlemen*, Borowski includes a short reference to the Auschwitz *Puff* (brothel) from the privileged male prisoner's point of view. Although the normality of mass murder and prisoner complicity in the system is often treated ironically as a moral issue in these stories, Borowski's prisoners consider the brothel to be simply a pocket of normal life; the prostitutes are "treated like normal women with whom one talks of love and family."[47] The prostitutes represent women to the men, who seem universally obsessed with making contact with them, but the woman's point of view is not considered. *House of Dolls* is a novel narrated through the consciousness of various prisoners, including Jewish girls compelled to become prostitutes for German soldiers in order to survive.[48] The fear and degradation are convincingly portrayed, but the two main female characters tend toward stereotypes of naivete and fearless competence. Few male written memoirs deal with a male inmate faced with the choice of providing sex for food. One of these rarities is Eugen Heimler's *Night of the Mist,* where the narrator accepts a sexual liaison with a gypsy girl in order to keep a privileged job as the assistant of her *kapo* father.[49] Male prisoners, however, do not portray themselves as being subjected to sexual assault by the SS or punished for refusing prostitution.

In Holocaust literature there is a variety of themes subsumed under the terms "sexual abuse" and "sexual assault." These synonymous terms are used here to signify any form of coercive sexual activity or threat in the literature. Besides direct forms, coercive sexual activity includes indirect forms like punishment for refusing prostitution, verbal sexual humiliation, and the threat of sexual coercion.

Sexual violence figures prominently in ghettos and the early stages of camp life. Aichinger, Schaeffer, Klein, and Dribben deal extensively with occupation and/or ghetto stages. Only Aichinger's novel about children refrains from this theme. The most thorough treatment of the theme occurs in *Anya*, where the possibility of capture for the German soldiers' brothels threatens Anya almost immediately after the Germans invade Vilno. This threat establishes her vulnerability as a woman apart from being a Jew because she has blond hair and an "Aryan" appearance. In this situation, Schaeffer shows the survival value of her willingness to take risks when she goes out on the streets in search of food for her family. The fear of rape accompanies the protagonist quite convincingly throughout the varied phases of her ordeal.

A radically different treatment of sexual violence occurs at the beginning of Judith Dribben's memoir, which takes place early during the Nazi occupation of Lvov, her home city in Poland.[50] Dribben enacts the role of sexual temptress to lure Nazi officers to their deaths in a partisan headquarters. Dribben's attractiveness as a weapon of resistance is plausible since she has blond hair, a non-Jewish appearance, ample aggressiveness and intelligence.

The camp initiation period typically includes some kind of sexual humiliation. Verbal abuse occurs in the memoirs by Dribben and Fénelon, and in the novel *Anya*. In the novel, SS "physicians" humiliate the new arrivals both physically and verbally.

"So," said one approaching me, "lice, eh?" He pinched my nipples. "And how is this after the trip, all dirty, eh?" He pulled at my pubic hair. I could hear Sonya next to me breathing in terrified little gasps. My stomach was heaving and heaving. . . . "Gasoline for you," he said, "for the lice," and then the next man came along and it began again. My breasts were so sore I could feel the pain in my toes."[51]

Sexual verbal insults during the camp initiation period assault a woman's sexual identity and thus speed up the process of destroying her feelings of self-worth. The term "whore" is one of the first and most common insults applied against female deportees, even by female *kapos*. During the initiation in Dribben's memoir, a *kapo* beats a white-haired Italian woman to unconsciousness for no reason, shouting "*Disgraziata putana* (disgraceful whore)," as if the woman's guilt were thus established. Another traumatic moment of initiation into a camp is the complete shaving of Jewish women. Many memoirists have commented on this trauma as it symbolizes the loss in a concrete way of a woman's socially defined identity. Livia Jackson describes the resulting depersonalization vividly: "a blank, senseless stare emerges on a thousand faces of one naked, unappealing body."[52] But she also asserts the possibility to adjust rather rapidly: both she and her mother continue to see each other as beautiful. Fénelon feels only overwhelming anger at the Polish functionaries who taunt her with her chopped-off braids.

Neither Dribben nor Klein describes any sexual abuse during

the initiation stage. Both of them enter their very different camps as privileged prisoners, Dribben as a political prisoner into Birkenau (she conceals her Jewishness) and Klein as a skilled laborer into Bolkenhain, a German labor camp. However, both of them later suffer a reversal of fate so that their status drops dangerously. As a result, both Dribben and Klein are on one occasion presented with the choice between prostitution and likely death.

In these two memoirs, the women's defiance of the option of prostitution leads to the punishment of *Strafkommando* work. This penal work represents the camp experience at its worst: back-breaking manual labor, floggings, sadistic SS who loose their brutal dogs on prisoners for the pleasure of inflicting punishment. The parallel aspects of these two narratives suggest that the effects of targeting for sexual abuse and prostitution are not uncommon, whether the prisoner accepts or refuses sex for improved food.

In each of these works, the protagonist's confrontation with sexual assault reverses an overall tendency of character portrayal, either as heroic or non-heroic. For example, Judith Dribben is the most traditionally heroic of all the writers treated. Her streetwalker disguise is the first of a series of strong partisan disguises which help her defeat the enemy. Her Russian spy disguise screens her Jewishness and makes her entry into Auschwitz a privileged one. But her Russian disguise backfires when she is punished with a group of other Russians for a collective refusal to submit to prostitution in a camp brothel. The *Strafkommando* work reduces all to the same level, struggling against heavy physical exertion, cold, and indiscriminate beatings not to become "Muslims" (candidates ready for the crematoria). "We walked with frozen legs and feet in our worn-out shoes . . . the effort required of us was enormous."[53] Only severe illness and life-saving injections organized by friends allow Judith to escape the fate of death for resisting prostitution.

Gerda Klein's resistance against a supervisor's demand for sex is a personal rather than a collective act, and it almost kills her. He condemns her to days loading flax bundles, coupled with nights loading coal. "I knew now what the supervisor meant when he said, 'You will be sorry.' . . . The same never-ending day continued and melted into the night and coal."[54] Like Dribben, her release from near-fatal hard labor is accomplished by the help of a friend. In this case, the most unusual aspect of the ordeal is Ilse's intervention, for this extremely timid girl acts courageously at great personal risk. On a later occasion, a threat of selections for a soldiers' brothel leads Gerda to buy poison, although she has promised her father never to take her own life.

The similarity of the situations in Klein and Dribben suggest that resisting the threat of sexual assault results in survival only through the help of friends and luck. Resistance results in more intense forms of hard labor which are intended to lead to a quicker annihilation. These situations have a leveling effect on different types of prisoners.

A different kind of response to the equation of sex and survival is described in *Playing for Time*. As in Dribben's memoir, the possibility of sexual assault threatens the pose of resistance which the narrator-protagonist emphasizes. However, rather than threatening the resistance of the central figure, in Fénelon the victim is another character who begins as her friend and ends as everyone's enemy. While two orchestra women have sexual liaisons with *kapos*, Clara's case represents the most dramatic transformation from innocence to evil under the pressure of the camp system. The trade of sexual favors for food appears as a free act; the only hidden coercion is Clara's excessive dependence on food, the one point at which life in the orchestra is as impoverished as life for the ordinary inmates. At first, the reader sympathizes with this pampered rich little girl confronted by the harshness of Birkenau; then as she passes from *kapo*'s whore to sadistic *kapo* in her own right, the reader, more alienated, witnesses the outward manifestation of the process by which victim turns into victimizer.[55] Clara acts as a foil for Fania and others, whose collaboration with the reigning powers is strictly musical but worrisome enough to motivate self-justification. Clara is an image of the dehumanizing process of Birkenau, as well as one of several motives for Fénelon's typical self portrayal as moral guide and judge of her sister inmates.

Sexual assault by non-Nazis in Holocaust works often tends to be an expression of victory in battle by the victorious armies. Liberated female deportees experience or fear rape by liberating armies, especially Russians, in such memoirs as those by Judith

Dribben, Reska Weiss, Margarete Buber, and Judith Sternberg Newman. Frequently there is an erotic side to the meeting of male liberators and female inmates. This is idealized in Fénelon, Schaeffer, and Klein, but it is highly ironic in Judith Dribben and other memoirs where the Allied soldier turns out to be a rapist. In *A Girl Called Judith Strick,* the survivor learns of the fatal raping of a camp comrade by American soldiers who thought they had been prostitutes serving the Germans and betraying their country. While fighting as a tank machine gunner in the Soviet battle of Vienna, Dribben witnesses a Russian soldier rape a woman. Silent about her true feelings, she half reveals her disgust at her comrades in her description of the rape and the defensive remarks of her commander, who attributes the reputation for rape of the Russian army to the "backward minorities." The incident is one of the few which divides Dribben from anti-Nazi men, with whom she usually identifies to a high degree.

How the fear of rape influences the survivor's relations to potential helpers is well developed in *Anya.* Anya frequently gets help from men who constitute a sexual threat, often imaginary but no less frightening. The novel implies that, while a woman can benefit from sexual attractiveness to survive, it is difficult for her to distinguish between the real allies and exploiters.

A discussion of sexual brutality in women's Holocaust narratives would be incomplete without some mention of the sadistic SS women. In most Holocaust works surveyed which are by women, the erotic face of brutality is at least partly female. Lina Wertmüller has popularized the "rape" of a male prisoner by a female commandant who exacts sex as the price of survival in the film "Seven Beauties." Such power of a woman over a man is highly improbable in a men's concentration camp, where all power rested with men.

However, the Nazi system placed many sexually disturbed people, females and males, in positions of power in concentration camps. In many Holocaust works by women, female sadism plays a role, showing that the Nazi system allowed equal opportunity to women and men in the exercise of sexual brutality over captive women.

Many memoirs of female inmates of Birkenau mention the

ferocious sadism of beautiful SS woman Irma Grese. Both Fania Fénelon and Judith Dribben refer to her "angelic" face and blond hair, a female embodiment of beauty and cruelty to stand beside the likes of Dr. Mengele and Maria Mandel. Dribben describes her in a state of sexual arousal at the sight of dogs tearing the bodies of two girls at a *Strafkommando* site. "The sight of the blood seemed to intoxicate her. She panted. She was sexually excited—everybody could see that. We stood in a trance, as at a gladiatorial combat."[56] Women's memoirs have a privileged view of the use of sex as an instrument of terror by females, since female SS were absent from the men's camps. Fénelon mentions the inmates' fear of Irma Grese's "unusually meticulous ferocity" of which a whiplash on the nipples was the smallest of her attentions.[57]

Some writers have exploited the sensationalism of lesbianism combined with brutality in the camps. The male writer Ka-Tzetnik 135633 uses demonic imagery in his novel *House of Dolls* to describe the ugly "Master-Kalefactress" of the Doll House (brothel) who takes sexual possession of her female victims in a diabolical ritual, like "a python about to entwine its prey," to cleanse the girl from sinful contact with a man.[58] In a somewhat different vein, Dribben seems as offended by the homosexuality of a hated *kapo* in Hirtenberg, a satellite camp of Mauthausen, as of her brutality. "She wanted to be an *Anweiserin* in Auschwitz, but they caught her—excuse me, it will disgust you—they caught her making love to a woman, another whore like herself."[59] Fénelon portrays Irma Grese as the terror that she was without implying that her homosexuality was the chief source of her evil. Unlike Dribben, for example, she is open-minded enough to treat sympathetically a positive lesbian relationship between two previously heterosexual orchestra members.[60]

Conclusion

Maternity, fertility, and sexual assault, experiences of relevance to women at all times, have a special importance in Holocaust literature by women. These themes do not, of course, exhaust the ghetto and camp experiences that women describe, but they do suggest certain aspects of it which outline an area of uniqueness to women. Because mothers were especially threatened and because a future for European Jews seemed unlikely to many camp inmates, narratives tend to place a high value on motherhood and fertility. In the context of mass death and compulsory sterility, the association of women with reproduction and the preservation of life gives them unique torments and, sometimes, forms of resistance. The female reproductive anatomy and roles seem particularly well suited to expressing some kinds of loss and biological survival in Holocaust literature.

The four texts which treat sexual abuse directly show that women's sexuality constitutes an additional method of Nazi persecution in certain settings. While one does not find many characters in memoirs engaging in prostitution, statements of many narrators suggest that in conditions of starvation, traditional sexual moral standards for females often became irrelevant. The examination of these narratives can correct overly simplistic judgements about the absence of sexuality among starving camp inmates.

Women's Holocaust literature often reveals the special confluence between women's attractiveness, customary female grooming, and a system in which survival sometimes depended upon appearance. The great emphasis on appearance in women's Holocaust narratives reflects both the specific function of looks in the camps as a basis for selecting prisoners to live or die and the traditional preoccupation of women with beauty. Since passing as a non-Jew was a far greater option for females than males (circumcision marked Jewish males), some women's survivor narratives feature exploiting blond hair as a survival strategy.

The Holocaust as an attack on femininity: certainly many will feel this view to be an intolerably sexist narrowing of perspective for a historical cataclysm. But narrowing the field of vision on an object brings something into sharper focus while it excludes something else. And the evidence from memoirs and the historical record shows that women are often attacked in terms of their specific biological functions. Such traditional forms of attacking females as rape continue despite the supposedly higher priority of maintaining racial purity. Domination and exploitation seem more consistently applied to inmates than racial the-

ories. As Anna Pawełczyńska cryptically states, the main purpose of sexual distinctions in the Nazi persecutions had the
function of providing extra opportunities for torturing and killing prisoners. By uncovering some of the torments specific to
women, one achieves something unintended but quite valuable:
details of a specific experience give form and substance to the
general experience because concreteness is more compelling
than generality. Particularly with regard to mothers and children, the depiction of ordinary women forced to choose between
their children's and their own immediate deaths must be among
the most grotesque and painful experiences in Holocaust literature. The theme of amenorrhea shows the extent to which the
expectation of genocide must have been present, with the widespread fear of permanent infertility to plague survivors.

Ultimately the feminist significance of women's Holocaust
texts is that they are as representative of the general Holocaust
experience as men's texts. Like the narratives of men, they represent the specific forms of suffering of one sex, the unique
experiences of an individual, and universal aspects of the Holocaust experience.

Notes

1. Mary Ellman, *Thinking About Women* (New York: Harcourt, Brace,
and World, 1968), pp. 71–72.

2. Anna Pawełczyńska, *Values and Violence in Auschwitz* (Berkeley
and Los Angeles: University of California Press, 1979), p. 53.

3. Cynthia Haft, *The Theme of Nazi Concentration Camps in French
Literature* (The Hague, Paris: Mouton, 1973), p. 121.

4. Pawełczyńska, pp. 53–54.

5. Joan Miriam Ringelheim, "The Unethical and the Unspeakable:
Women and the Holocaust," *Simon Wiesenthal Center Annual* 1, p. 72
(based on conversation with Raul Hilberg).

6. Vera Laska, *Women in the Resistance and in the Holocaust: The Voices
of Eyewitnesses* (Westport, Conn.: Greenwood Press, 1983), p. 7; Nadine
Brozan, "Holocaust Women: A Study in Survival," *New York Times*,
March 23, 1983, pp. C–1, 16; Esther Katz and Joan Miriam Ringelheim,
Proceedings of the Conference Women Surviving the Holocaust (New York:
The Institute for Research in History, 1983), p. 63.

7. Gerald Reitlinger, *Final Solution*, 2nd rev. and augm. ed. (South Brunswick, N.J.: T. Yoseloff, 1961), p. 118.

8. Jacob Apenszlak, ed., *The Black Book of Polish Jewry* (New York: Roy Publishers, 1943), p. 247.

9. Gisella Perl, *I Was a Doctor in Auschwitz* (Salem, N. H.: Ayer Company, 1984), p. 86.

10. Ella Lingens-Reiner, *Prisoners of Fear* (London: Victor Gollancz, 1948), pp. 61–62.

11. Germaine Tillion, *Ravensbrück* (Garden City, N. Y.: Doubleday, 1975), pp. 101–2; Margarete Buber, *Under Two Dictators*, trans. Edward Fitzgerald (New York: Dodd, Mead, and Company, 1949), p. 306.

12. Apenszlak, pp. 25–29.

13. Raul Hilberg, *Destruction of the European Jews* (Chicago: Quadrangle, 1961), p. 28.

14. *The Black Book: The Nazi Crime Against the Jewish People* (New York: The Jewish Black Book Committee, 1946), pp. 301, 329, 340; *Trial of the Major War Criminals Before the International Military Tribunal*, Vol. 7, (Nuremberg, 1947), pp. 456–57.

15. Katz and Ringelheim, *Proceedings*, p. 47.

16. Ruth Alton (Tauber), *Deportiert von den Nazis* (unpublished manuscript, Leo Baeck Institute, 1961).

17. Laska, p. 27.

18. Gertrud Scholz-Klink, "Weg und Aufgabe der national-sozialistischen Frauenbewegung," in Ellen Semmelroth and Renate von Stieda, eds., *N. S. Frauenbuch* (Munich: J. F. Lehmanns Verlag, 1934), p. 15; Kate Millett, *Sexual Politics* (Garden City, N.Y.: Doubleday, 1970), p. 165; Clifford Kirkpatrick, *Nazi Germany: Its Women and Family Life* (Indianapolis: Bobbs-Merrill Co., 1938), p. 116; Wilhelm Reich, *The Mass Psychology of Fascism* (New York: Farrar, Straus, and Giroux, 1970), p. 106; F. Lenz, "Zur Frage der unehelichen Kinder," *Volk und Rasse* 12 (March 1, 1937), 91 ff.; Herbert Kussmann, *Die Familie und das Erbe* (Berlin-Schoeneberg: Langenscheidtsche Verlagsbuchhandlung, 1935), pp. 25–26.

19. Adolf Hitler, *Mein Kampf*, trans. Ralph Mannheim (Boston: Houghton Mifflin Co., 1943), p. 228.

20. Ibid., p. 55.

21. Ibid., p. 295.

22. Fania Fénelon, *Playing for Time* (New York: Atheneum, 1977), pp. 88–89.

23. Gerda Klein, *All But My Life* (New York: Hill and Wang, 1957), p. 177. See also Katz and Ringelheim, *Proceedings*, p. 137, for testimony about the permanent loss of fertility.

24. Fénelon, p. 88.

25. Livia Bitton Jackson, *Elli* (New York: Times Books, 1980), p. 86.

26. Sidra Ezrahi, *By Words Alone: The Holocaust in Literature* (Chicago: The University of Chicago Press, 1980), p. 71.

27. Charlotte Delbo, *None of Us Will Return*, trans. John Githens (New York: Grove Press, 1968), pp. 106–7. (Original title: *Aucun de nous ne reviendra* (Paris: Editions Gonthier, 1965.)

28. William Newton Stephens, "A Cross-Cultural Study of Menstrual Taboos," *Genetic Psychology Monographs* 64 (1961), pp. 397, 398, 402; M. Esther Harding, *Woman's Mysteries* (New York: Harper Colophon Books, 1976), pp. 56–63, 72–73.

29. Janice Delaney, Mary Jane Lupton, Emily Toth, *The Curse: A Cultural History of Menstruation* (New York: The New American Library, 1976), p. 67.

30. Norma Rosen, *Touching Evil* (New York: Harcourt, Brace and World, 1969), pp. 86, 131.

31. Susan Fromberg Schaeffer, *Anya* (New York: Avon Books, 1976), p. 267.

32. See also Ruth Alton-Tauber's memoir *Deportiert von den Nazis* about a mother in the Lodz ghetto (unpub. ms., Leo Baeck Institute).

33. Delbo, *None of Us Will Return*, p. 9.

34. Ibid., p. 44.

35. Ibid., p. 72–73.

36. Ibid., p. 73.

37. As used by Terrence Des Pres in *The Survivor*, "extremity" refers to the condition of life in the Nazi death camps, and despite some differences, in the Soviet camps. It signifies "a world, finally, in which an anti-human order is maintained by the bureaucratic application of death . . . spiritual vacuum, physical anguish and empty time." (Oxford, New York: Oxford University Press, 1976), pp. 11, 13.

38. Schaeffer, p. 275.

39. Ibid., pp. 386 ff.

40. Fénelon, p. 225.

41. Ilona Karmel, *An Estate of Memory* (Boston: Houghton Mifflin, 1969).

42. Judith Sternberg Newman, *In the Hell of Auschwitz* (New York: Exposition, 1964), p. 43; Olga Lengyel, *Five Chimneys: The Story of Auschwitz* (Chicago: Ziff-Davis, 1947), p. 100.

43. Reska Weiss, *Journey Through Hell* (London: Vallentine, Mitchell, 1961), p. 185.

44. Fénelon, p. 252.

45. Ibid., p. 158.

46. Pawełczyńska, p. 99.

47. Tadeusz Borowski, *This Way for the Gas, Ladies and Gentlemen* (New York: Penguin, 1967), p. 109.

48. Ka-Tzetnik 135633, *House of Dolls*, trans. Moshe M. Kohn (London: Frederick Muller Ltd., 1956). This author's pseudonym refers to the German letters "K.Z.," the abbreviation for Konzentrationslager (concentration camp). Each camp inmate ("Ka-Tzetnik") was known by the number tattooed on the left arm.

49. Eugen Heimler, *Night of the Mist*, trans. Andre Ungar (Westport, Conn.: Greenwood, 1978), pp. 49–53, 62–63.

50. Judith Dribben, *A Girl Called Judith Strick* (New York: Cowles Book Company, 1970), pp. 4–8.

51. Schaeffer, p. 280.

52. Jackson, p. 71.

53. Dribben, p. 202.

54. Klein, p. 150.

55. Fénelon, p. 245.

56. Dribben, p. 206.

57. Fénelon, p. 83.

58. Ka-Tzetnik, p. 174.

59. Dribben, p. 222.

60. Fénelon, pp. 141–51. The fate of deported lesbians is still essentially unknown. They were not persecuted officially as were the male homosexuals. See Vera Laska, *Women in the Resistance and in the Holocaust*, pp. 23–25; Frank Rector, *The Nazi Extermination of Homosexuals* (New York: Stein and Day, 1981), p. 115; and Renate Bridenthal et al., *When Biology Became Destiny: Women in Weimar and Nazi Germany* (New York: Monthly Review Press, 1984), p. 330 n. 100.

II

CHARACTERIZATION IN HOLOCAUST NARRATIVES

When some critics of concentration camp literature refer to characterization in the texts they are discussing, they describe a sameness of character from one narrative to another. These tend to follow a predictable sequence of events, which impose limits on the development of character. The camps offer encounters with a finite range of events and people, and consequently memoirs about them reveal only certain facets of personality. For example, Barbara Foley recalls the nearly identical torpor and passivity reported to be experienced by a mature doctor (Elie Cohen) and a teenaged girl (Gerda Klein) as they entered their respective camps.[1] Even in accounts of resistance to the process of self dissolution, aimed at by the camps, Foley notes typed rather than particularized responses. While these remarks have a general validity, the closer examination of Holocaust memoirs reveals much greater differentiation. This is especially true if one examines accounts featuring different types of work. The camp labor hierarchy provided quite different opportunities for suffering or evading exhausting work, beatings, starvation, and exposure to the elements. Holocaust memoirs are also often affected by differences in the present-time situation of the writer, which help to determine how the past will be recreated. While the resulting characters often lack the detailed development of ordinary autobiographical personalities, they exhibit some key differences when compared with each other.

In lieu of individualized characters, Holocaust critics have distinguished three types: the survivor, the victim, and the hero. The survivor refuses his/her condition as victim by engaging in a strategy for personal survival and by retaining a modified code of morals. In the camps, inmates had to let go of many of their former moral standards in order to survive. The survivor's identity depends more upon the struggle to maintain life in a system of death by an accretion of small acts of defiance than it does on actual biological survival, an outcome much dependent on factors beyond the individual's control. In other words, the survivor is defined by an attitude and set of actions while living in extremity, however long or short the duration.[2]

The victim is distinguished from the survivor in more than one way. Sidra Ezrahi compares the victim to the cannibal, arguing that inmates who acquiesce to the brutality of the camp system become its victims, even if they survive.[3] Another version of the victim is (in camp lingo) the *Muslim*, *Musulman*, or *Schmückstück*, those inmates who succumbed to shock and especially starvation either soon after arrival or later. They became listless, obedient, walking automatons, and quickly died. Camp survivors estimate the camp survival period of the totally obedient inmate, i.e., one who did not "organize" extra food and necessities by stealing from the camp, as three months maximum. Many accounts refer to these victims as a background to the main narrative, part of the camp landscape, or as a feared fate for the main characters.

The survivor is also distinguished from the hero, almost invariably from the tragic or sacrificial hero. Traditional heroism invariably involves an individual exemplary death, but in a universe bent on the death of millions, individual death counts for too little to be a significant gesture. Victory over this system is moral survival with sanity intact, while dying is merely capitulation. However, the over-narrow focussing of criticism on heroic death leaves out other forms of heroism which many authors and readers find more appropriate. In an environment of death, the act of helping another person to live could reach heroic proportions if measured by such criteria as risk and resistance to the prevailing death and moral degeneration. Holocaust memoirists offer many examples of such responses but vary in the extent to which they emphasize the heroic aspect of them.

Despite the restrictions of camp experiences, when Holocaust memoirs are compared with each other, they often exhibit different ways of handling typical Holocaust experiences. Rather than only one survivor character, there are several. Holocaust memoirs are narrations by survivors about other survivors and victims and often use fictional techniques. Some of the more convincing Holocaust novels are fictional imitations of Holocaust memoirs, exploiting first-person narrators and other autobiographical conventions. Whether actually autobiographical or fictional, all these narrators tell their stories for apparently different purposes and employ different kinds of survivor types in the process.

An efficient way to show the existence of different survivor characters is to pick a typical camp experience described in most texts and to see how survivors respond to the experience. Being beaten, a common event in many memoirs, requires submitting temporarily to a condition of additional powerlessness but also offers possibilities for distancing in the retelling of the event. The ways in which characters distance themselves from such painful situations in their memoirs shows that they reject the state of pure victimization in a variety of ways. Authors of survivor narratives, either their own stories or those of others, deal with aspects of victimization but also somehow transcend it. We will look at the techniques of self-portrayal of protagonists or another character being beaten, including images and the emotions conveyed.

Charlotte Delbo, Susan F. Schaeffer, and Gerda Klein present their protagonists in beating scenes which convey suffering with considerable intensity. The first two use images of animals to indicate their dehumanization: Delbo refers to the inmates working under blows as "pitiable defenseless insects" and Anya refers to her painful climb into bed after her beating as that of "a crab missing a leg" and her buttocks as a turtle shell.[4] Klein describes her demoralization more directly: "the blows . . . shattered the wall of strength that I had built for myself. Survive? All of a sudden it did not seem worthwhile."[5]

While all these images communicate victimization, the narrators reveal their helplessness and moderate it by means of various strategies. Gerda Klein expresses her vulnerability by conveying the assailant as an anonymous impersonal force which not only disfigures her body but also causes the shrinking of her sensory awareness.

I felt a heavy blow over my eyes. "Who?" he demanded. "I don't know," I repeated. Another blow fell, deafening my left ear. I swayed and staggered toward the building. When I finally reached my bunk I sat there without undressing. My face was puffed and bruised, my skin and lips were moist with blood. I must have cried without knowing it.[6]

The incident has the quality of a confession when it is contrasted to the vow made five pages earlier, after another inmate is beaten, that she will strike back if she is beaten, regardless of the danger. However, Klein moderates the impression of personal weakness by asserting that this beating represents the hardest trial for her in the camps—worse than hunger or hard work. Further she follows this incident with a distraction: her girlfriend, unaware of the beating, presents to her a slightly mashed raspberry on a leaf.

Like Klein's depersonalized falling blows, the identity of the attacker in Schaeffer's *Anya* remains a background shadow. In the foreground remains only the carefully described whip and then the sensory reality of physical pain, like a crazed creature trying to escape the blows:

Turning my head, I could see him take the leather tongues, five of them knotted together at the handle, flying loose like tails; he was dipping them in the water that collected under the dripping faucet. . . . The pain pushed at the top of my head and my toes like something alive trying to get out. Then I stopped screaming. When I got up I could hardly walk.[7]

Schaeffer's technique depends frequently on similes to make extreme suffering available to the reader's imagination but also to convey detachment from pain. Her narrator Anya resorts to humor and conversation as distractions against the pathos of her condition. After the beating, she describes climbing to her bunk, "slowly, like a crab missing a leg." Seeing Anya's black bottom, her friend Rachel whispers "in an awed voice" that it will take a long time to heal. Anya replies that she will sleep on her belly with her "shell in the air like a turtle."[8] Almost immediately, she is distracted by the letter she has sent to her child's benefactor.

Both the depersonalization noted in Klein and Schaeffer and the anonymity of the attacker in Klein extend with greater force to a group of prisoners in Charlotte Delbo's lyrical memoir *None of Us Will Return.* Surreal images of body parts represent outdoor workers beaten in repetitive images which convey intense suffering through accretion in a timeless present. "All along the way clubs on the back of the neck, switches on the temples, straps on the kidneys. Screams. Screams. Screams that scream to the invisible limits of the marsh."[9] Delbo employs an unusual strategy for a personal memoir: she often includes herself only as an unnamed member of the mass of inmates, designated as "we." "We try to protect our faces, our eyes. The blows fall on the backs of our necks, on our backs. Schnell. Schnell. Run."[10] Delbo's images evoke visual, tactile, and auditory stimuli to draw the reader into a world of continuous blows and running. Delbo's main form of distancing is the concealment of the personal suffering of the narrator within the "we."

Each of the three texts discussed above has narrators who project themselves as suffering victims while being beaten. In each case, the victim distances herself personally from that suffering. Klein is the most objective but distances herself through reflection about lesser ordeals and the distraction of her friend's gift. Anya, like Klein, concentrates on the personal experience of a single beating but detaches herself and the reader through humor and other thoughts. Both texts describe only one beating and isolate it from the rest of the narrative. Delbo erases the personal completely, leaving a surreal portrait of suffering body parts.

Despite the variations in distancing devices in the three texts, the experience of being beaten is primarily one of suffering. But not all narratives convey beatings in this way. The narrators of Fania Fénelon's and Judith Dribben's memoirs portray themselves differently when they describe similar situations. Like Schaeffer and Klein, they personalize the ordeal, but they handle the reactions of the suffering protagonist in a different way. Fania Fénelon reports two beatings in her memoir, *Playing for Time*. Shortly after her arrival in Birkenau, she mentions a beating for emptying a pail of dirty water outside. A little later she describes the earlier beating she receives in prison after arrest for resistance activities.

Tears of rage, mingled with blood, trailed down my grubby cheeks. I wiped the tears away with the back of my hand and huddled up against Clara, whose warmth afforded some comfort.

"Did they find out your real name?" "No. In the end I gave it to them. I was tired of being beaten—it's oddly monotonous." . . . "How did they beat you?" "With an iron bar, on my back."[11]

These passages reveal reactions absent from the passages discussed so far: anger in the first one, and the denial of pain in the second. By means of these responses, Fénelon transforms her status from that of a victim to an opponent. Fénelon suppresses the actual experience and its pain and belittles the beating in prison by revealing only the boredom of it. Yet she reveals that an iron bar was used on her back, thereby implying her stoicism. She even denies her torturers the power to extract her real name, maintaining that she "gave it to them."

The projection of anger and invulnerability is characteristic for Judith Dribben as well. She describes several of her sessions with police interrogators in a Polish prison in martial terms. She fights blows with insults and implies victory.

"I have nothing to confess. And get rid of this dirty liar." "Take care of her," the Gestapo man ordered. The civilian began punching my head and face and kicking me with his boots. A beating hurts your body, but even more it hurts your human pride. I was so angry I hardly felt the blows. I poured out on them all the insults I had ever heard in my life. "Stop," the Gestapo man ordered.[12]

Even more than Fania Fénelon, Dribben minimizes her suffering while maximizing her anger despite a severe beating. Amazingly, she asserts that her anger dulls her awareness of pain, and her insults are followed by a temporary end to the beatings. Thus she implies that she is the winner of the match. Physical suffering is unimportant. At one point, she mentions the loss of three teeth and pains all over her body from hard kicks but then restores her image of invulnerability when a doctor asks her why she does not complain. "It wouldn't be dignified," she replies.[13]

The denial of physical suffering in both Dribben and Fénelon is quite unlike the attention to the physical in the first three writers. In this way and through the expression of anger, they create a self-dramatizing portrayal which minimizes their vulnerability and idealizes their resistance to physical brutality. However, they forfeit some claims to credibility by means of this pose and seem to be conveying too many present-day concerns about insufficient Jewish resistance in the past.

A similar imposition of external values upon narrated events is found in Ilse Aichinger's novel, *Herod's Children*. Here the denial of physical suffering increases as a mystical perspective defines the experience of being beaten as insignificant. The main protagonist, Ellen, a half-Jewish girl, never suffers a beating from Nazi officials and is in general less victimized than most of the other characters discussed. However, in one scene another character who has been beaten interacts with Ellen. During Ellen's interrogation because of suspected resistance activity, one of her Jewish friends is thrown quite unexpectedly at her feet:

Before she could get hold of herself, a wet, bloody mass fell at her feet. . . . "But somebody gave me away, Ellen, and then they found me. They dragged me out from under the bed and down the stairs. He's the one, that one over there . . . " "He's asleep," said Ellen disdainfully. "He's missing, disappeared, but he doesn't know it. They find everyone else, but they've all lost themselves."[14]

In this passage, suffering and the denial of suffering are divided between two characters, Bibi as the victim and Ellen as the vehicle for anger and stoicism. Ellen's contemptuous dismissal of the guard who has found Bibi is typical of the kind of spiritual resistance marshalled in the novel against Nazi violence. Ellen persuades Bibi to accept the fate of deportation, which in this Christian novel is victory over the illusory world of the living. Thus Bibi, through her choice, also changes from pure victim to a kind of victor over circumstance. Although there is initially some indication of real brutality in "a wet, bloody mass," it is made insignificant by the weight of spiritual transcendence in Ellen's rhetoric. As in Dribben and Fénelon, anger and the denial that brutality is real are the tools of the self-dramatizing protagonist, but here the degree of denial is much greater.

A memoir which provides a more moderate version of spiritual transcendence of suffering is Livia Bitton Jackson's *Elli*. The thirteen-year-old Hungarian Jewish girl survives a beating in Auschwitz, a punishment for pushing an SS woman away from her sick mother. Jackson does not spare the reader much of the harshness of the attack. Her body's protective numbness mitigates the impression of suffering somewhat.

The punch on my cheek sends me reeling. A second punch knocks me to the slippery floor. Then she is on top of me, kicking me in the face, in the chest, in the abdomen. The black boots gleam and my blood splashes thinly on the wet floor. A final kick sends me rolling across the floor toward the exit. Then the door slams and I am lying numb on the cold slippery floor.[15]

The transcendence of the beating stems not from a denial of pain (the body deals with pain on its own), but from the fact of survival itself and the narrator's recognition of the improbability of this outcome. Her subsequent description is predominantly a prayer to celebrate this victory, an implied miracle, particularly in the context of the memoir's other more explicit references to miracles. "Then a thought formulates somehow—I am alive! I taste blood. I am unable to lift my head. My body feels totally numb. But I am alive. She did not trample me to death. She could have shot me. But she did not."[16] Since the beating is described as a punishment for an inmate's attack, "the gravest form of sabotage," the significance of not paying for the sabotage with death looms larger in importance than the suffering. Victimization is thus once again made insignificant.

To summarize, the characterization of victims of beatings in the six works functions by means of two basic patterns. Emphasis on the body, comparison with animals, the evocation of suffering, and depersonalization are all stylistic techniques which convey victimization and self-effacement to varying degrees. This suffering is distanced and mitigated by undercutting through humor and other distractions. Schaeffer, Klein, and Delbo all exploit a self-effacing strategy and in the process produce a mimetic (in Northrop Frye's terminology) version of the concentration camp experience. However, not all Holocaust narratives follow this pattern. Others, such as those by Dribben, Fénelon, Aichinger, and Jackson, emphasize the spiritual and the human rather than the animal aspect of inmates: they stress the insignificance of suffering, the response of anger against the oppressor, the integrity of the person or the significance of survival. These are all techniques which create a self-dramatizing, resisting portrayal and a more idealized view of possibilities in the Holocaust.

The differing responses to beatings which have been described above are indicative of more global differences in Holocaust narratives. Based on the way the main protagonist responds typically to danger and suffering, these memoirs and novels seem to be either primarily stories of inexplicable survival against great odds or stories of successful resistance against the enemy. The narrators bear witness to different versions of the past—either survival as a combination of victimization and miraculous survival or resistance as a series of battles (usually verbal) in order to prove they have won something other than survival. The key difference is the present-time attitude of the narrator toward her own and often others' survival. In part due to the complexity of survival causes, which always include chance, the characterization of the survival narrative protagonist is often relatively self-effacing. On the other hand, the resistance story is typically told by a self-dramatizing protagonist, one who maximizes dignity and personal control over fate by demonstrating successful resistance. Even though a strong case could be made for the collective nature of many resistance activities, narratives about them often emphasize individual initiative and responsibility as part of an autobiographical strategy.

Self-Effacing Survivors

The narrators of Charlotte Delbo's *None of Us Will Return* and Susan Fromberg Schaeffer's *Anya* are both self-effacing survivors of survival narratives. The works differ in several significant ways such as genre, the intensity of evil shown to be threatening the protagonist, and the range of possible actions. In Delbo's work, a memoir composed of lyrical episodes which focus on the collective experience of Birkenau, the confrontations with Nazi officials generally involve beatings or death. In *Anya*, a work of fiction based on survivor testimony, and with a much wider historical panorama and range of possibilities, the protagonist is able at times to confront Nazis and other officials and to enhance her survival chances in this way. In both survival narratives, the protagonist responds to great danger at key moments with appropriate risk-taking actions which are part of the reason for her survival. Neither narrator emphasizes these actions in trying to account for survival. Delbo attributes her survival to the solidarity and assistance of the other deportees and to the power of latent survival mechanisms within her body. Anya emphasizes the role of a "superpower," which she also labels fate, with secondary help from the assistance of others, her mother's careful upbringing, and her youth and "Aryan" attractiveness. Because both protagonists ignore part of the evidence, namely their individual responsibility for the outcome, and neither one highlights her risky actions as ends in themselves, they have a self-effacing view of their respective survivals.

Delbo's self-effacement correlates appropriately to the greater extremity depicted in the work. Her apparent aim is to convey the horror of the death camp and the awesome struggle of the women inmates, especially the many who did not survive. Her personal story is often submerged within the collective, thus allowing her to reveal great suffering without calling attention to herself.

Delbo emphasizes the body as the representative locus of the struggle for survival. While psychological issues have some importance, they are not the most striking. Survival reduces to physical endurance, an outcome essentially resistant to logical explication. Delbo's self-effacing attitude to her individual effort is manifested in the episode in which she and three other women carry two corpses on boards from the marshes where they have worked back to camp, about five kilometers. The paradoxical combination of enormous effort and the decisiveness of physical strength independent of will is typical for Delbo's descriptions of inmate life in Birkenau. The will to continue stems from a desire to defy the laughter of the *kapos*. However, the successful exertion of will to carry the heavy burdens depends upon the continuation of the heartbeat, which cannot be willed, only witnessed:

Our hearts thump, thump as if they were to burst and we think: my heart will not stand it, I will have heart failure. It has not failed yet, it is still holding up. For how many yards? Our anxiety breaks up the miles into paces, yards, light poles, bends in the road.[17]

The passage conveys both the subordination of the will to the body and that of individual experience to that of the group. The heart-protagonist shifts from the collective "our hearts" to the personal "my heart" of each member of the group, which reasserts its collective identity in "our anxiety." The narrator implies her experience within the collective signalled by "we" and "our" without singling herself out. However, Delbo's collectivizing strategy both conceals and reveals the hidden strength of the narrator-protagonist. After repeated pleading by the four carriers, two other women replace the weakest carriers, but the narrator continues to say "we" in the remainder of the episode. Her endurance is concealed behind the language of collective suffering, but she implies that she is one of only two inmates to carry the corpses the entire distance without a replacement. (The number of carriers remains four throughout.)[18] Delbo's narrator generally claims less strength than other prisoners, especially friends who help her. Her self-effacing portrayal allows her to convey the intensity of suffering and to reject any notion of justification for her survival in place of many others.

Delbo's recollections of other experiences convey the survivor's conflict between the desire to assert her own responsibility for survival and the awareness that her conscious efforts are not decisive. Among the author's most memorable episodes are those which describe women standing in long roll calls in freezing wind and darkness or intense sunlight. The narrator describes the immense effort of the women just to continue standing, while confessing that unconscious forces are decisive in her case.

We stand motionless and the amazing thing is that we are still standing. Why? No one thinks "What is the use" or else does not say it. With our last bit of strength, we stand. I stand in the midst of my comrades and I think that if I return one day and want to explain this inexplicable thing, I will say: "I used to say to myself: you must stand, you must stand for the entire roll call. You must stand again today. It is because you will have stood again today that you will return, if you do return one day." And this will be false. I did not say anything to myself. I did not think anything. The will to resist no doubt lay in a much deeper and more secret mechanism which has since broken; I shall never know.[19]

By asserting that her will to resist lay in a "secret mechanism" somewhere in her body, Delbo refuses to celebrate her conscious will to survive. Yet her evident struggle takes her beyond the category of victim. Although it may be false that she told herself to stand again each day in order to return, it is true that this daily struggle was necessary for that return.

As in this passage, Delbo's self-effacing explanations of endurance are often the result of an interpretation of facts which could be seen differently. Whether to live or die is surprisingly often a matter of personal choice for a deportee, but Delbo shares the responsibility for this decision with others. Each dawn she overcomes her attraction to the idea of dying and thus escaping pain when she sees the new corpses carried away without dignity on a short stretcher made of branches, to be thrown on a heap of corpses. "Then I know that all those who pass pass for me, that all those who die die for me. I watch them go by and say no."[20] The expression of personal dignity which her decision also represents is concealed behind the debt which binds her to the dead. They are somehow responsible for her decision to go on, even though it is she who has decided.

While Delbo usually conceals her strength and effort within collective images of suffering, in a few instances she takes credit for individual action or effort. Intense thirst (a special torment of water-poor Birkenau) compels her to leave the work procession when it passes a stream so that she can get water, thus risking being caught by the guard and his dog. The effort requires running down a bank, breaking ice on the surface, running back, and getting to the line with the SS man and his dog in pursuit. The other marchers are too afraid or too weak to imitate it, and guilt is the price she must pay for the renewal of her own life forces. While Delbo implicitly gives herself credit for a significant risk, she limits the potential for a self-dramatizing portrayal because her act is a means to surviving the threat of extreme thirst (not an end in itself), and it is followed by the guilt feelings from drinking all the water herself. In Delbo's depiction of the terror of Birkenau, individual risk-taking actions constitute options. This and other incidents in *None of Us Will Return* increase the reader's sense that Delbo is strong both physically and psychically. Therefore, her predominantly self-minimizing interpretation of survival varies somewhat from the evidence.

The circumstances surrounding Delbo's arrest give insights into the author's selectivity in her account of Birkenau. Appended to the text of Delbo's memoir is the statement that she and her husband Georges Dudach were active in the Resistance, that the Nazis arrested them on March 2, 1942, and executed him on May 23. Rosette Lamont provides the additional fact that Dudach refused to work for the Nazis in exchange for his life.[21] In 1941 she had been safe in Buenos Aires, working as a secretary for theatre director Louis Jouvet, who was on tour. Upon reading of the execution of a friend in the Resistance, she chose to return to France. These events contain the potential for a more self-idealizing characterization, but Delbo does not exploit them in this way.[22] Only her loyalty to other members of the Resistance is echoed in her descriptions of inmate solidarity in Birkenau.

The physical and social factors by which Delbo explains her survival allow her to free herself of responsibility (guilt for being one of few survivors) without turning to a divine power. Delbo (a non-Jew) dispenses with God in an early episode addressed to Christians, "You who have wept for two thousand years/ for one who suffered three days and three nights."[23] Her prisoners undergo their longer agony without the benefit of a belief in resurrection or hope for the tears of the world. But many other survivor documents reflect an experience of the Holocaust as a test of belief, and sometimes this faith increases through the ordeal. The heroine of *Anya*, the eldest daughter of a secular Jewish family from Vilno, Poland, finds new faith in the process of surviving. This turning to God begins before the war when, warned by her father in time, she is spared a face-scarring attack by Vilno University fraternity men against female Jewish students.

The relationship of chance, divine intervention in human fate, and personal responsibility appears as a major theme in this novel. As a truncated *Bildungsroman* beginning in the heroine's adolescence, the novel integrates the issue into the education of the main character. Her atheistic father, Boris Savikin, sees fate as all-powerful, while her mother, Rebecca, believes in personal responsibility. The face-scarring episode begins Anya's belief in a superpower, i.e., her belief that she is protected from harm. The plot of the novel can be viewed as a pattern of lucky co-incidences or, as Anya chooses, as evidence for the intervention of divine protection. Before the Holocaust, Anya is lucky to escape death from a lightning storm, a horse accident, and a miscarriage. She is one of very few Jewish women to be admitted to the medical school in Vilno. In Kaiserwald labor camp her barrack is the only one in the area to escape destruction by a fire, and a Jew disguised as a German officer picks her out from all the others to be helped to escape. A well-timed departure saves her from arrest with the Rutkauskus family who are hiding Ninka, her daughter. All are killed except Ninka because a German officer saves her. Anya then survives the mining of a train by partisans. A series of men and women, both strangers and past acquaintances, turn up with help when she is most in need. The source of nearly all these stories is Anya herself, the remarkably credible narrator of the novel. Viewing the pattern of coincidences, she concludes, "Always I felt this hand over me."[24]

While living in Vilno under Nazi occupation, Anya does not mention the superpower, although she is continually responding to the terror with considerable risk, repeatedly surviving as she tries and sometimes succeeds in saving the lives of other family members. The best psychological explanation for this silence is that the superpower does not save the lives of many people in her large, close-knit family. First, her "saintly" father is killed; then her sister Vera, Vera's husband, her two brothers, sister-in-law, and a baby are taken in a raid; then her husband Stajoe is taken and shot, and finally at the time of deportation her singular mother, too old to be sent to work, is sent to the death lines.

Since Anya as narrator emphasizes her responsibility for surviving this period, her characterization at times approaches the level of self-dramatization. A good example is her role during a Gestapo raid on a building where most of her family has temporarily found privileged shelter. Anya saves herself, her mother, her daughter, and her girlfriend by means of a conversation with a Polish soldier guarding the building.

"Oh," I said, "I think you're a father too? What do you have, a boy or a girl?" "Two boys," he answered. "Do you have pictures?" I asked. I kept on talking. "Here they are," he said, pulling some out. "Oh, such beautiful children!" I said, forcing myself not to hurry. "Ours are hungry. We don't know how to get to Polanska Street; we don't live here. Can you tell me how to get to Polanska Street?"[25]

Anya's successful strategy depends upon her ability to play a role convincingly during a dangerous moment, her quick thinking, but also upon her blond hair, "Aryan" appearance, and maternal role. It is one of the most self-dramatizing moments in the narration, but no celebration follows the event, since at the same time Anya and her mother lose six family members.

During later stages of Anya's ordeal, while she is responsible only for herself and her daughter, she evokes the superpower more frequently, while acting as if under some mysterious command. In Kaiserwald, this power helps her escape selection for death by walking back to the safe line and hiding. "Then, as if an invisible hand pushed me violently, I turned and walked back to the first line. I felt my hands pushing the women aside, pushing myself through, crouching slightly behind two tall ones."[26] Afterwards, she interprets the "invisible hand" as a divine power which needs the help of individual action: " 'But it needs help,' I thought to myself, getting down and going over to Ann's to see what new things she might have brought back from the disinfectant machine."[27] Here, she links faith and initiative causally; because she believes in the superpower, she takes additional action. At other times, different language evokes apparently involuntary survival actions. After a false accusation of stealing in a hospital (following escape from Kaiserwald), Anya is interrogated. "Something" makes her search the room and recognize one of the examining officers, a Polish man who once flirted with her in a Warsaw cafe. She appeals to his humanity and sexual attractiveness, and he saves her.

In addition to these unwilled causes of survival actions, Anya's physical appearance plays a major role. By giving Anya both beauty and a non-Jewish appearance, Schaeffer suggests that both can be significant assets for a woman as well as magnets of specific kinds of danger. Since the selections for death are made on the basis of appearance, a heightened value is attached to female beauty and grooming compared to ordinary life. Anya's mother continually tells her to groom herself because "a woman must always look her best, especially in the worst circumstances."[28] However, both female attractiveness and non-Jewish features are equivocal values in the novel. While Anya's hair protects her from some persecution as a Jew, it makes her more vulnerable as a woman, since "Aryan" women in the novel are prime targets for forced prostitution and rape. (Nazis who would stay away from "race defilement" with a Jew would not have this obstacle with an "Aryan" woman.) Anya narrowly escapes rape several times but sometimes is helped by men attracted to her.

As in the incident with the Polish soldier discussed above, Anya's blond hair and attractiveness contribute to her self-effacing portrayal because of the uncertainty surrounding their effect on the success of survival actions. The asset of blond hair and physical attractiveness influences several other incidents, including the saving of Anya's daughter Ninka by leaving her on church steps outside the Vilno ghetto where she is found by Christians. Individual initiative is supported by "Aryan" appearance—a matter of luck—but exactly how important it is remains uncertain. A dark-haired Jewish child would have less of a chance to pass as an "Aryan" Pole. On the other hand, Rachel, Anya's girlfriend, survives in better health than Anya despite her dark features. But her survival is significantly linked to Anya's help.

Anya is a work of fiction which permits the leading character a far wider range of actions during the Holocaust than is open to the protagonist of *None of Us Will Return*. Delbo's self-effacing narrator has fewer unique personal achievements to hide because simply to stand, to run, or to work are exhausting collective ordeals in Birkenau. Anya escapes from a labor camp prior to the introduction of maximal security measures (such as tattooing numbers on prisoners and erecting electrically charged barbed wire). This factor makes the story of her escape feasible in a way that would not work for Delbo in Birkenau. Each time that Anya evades the Nazi machinery of destruction, the novel reinforces the alliance of initiative, luck, and "superpower." By describing her successful actions in her first-person narrative, she implicitly gives herself credit, but in making fate or God the most important reason, she establishes a self-effacing portrayal based upon a discrepancy between action and credit given. It is also implicitly based upon the difficulty of being the sole survivor of a large family, a situation for which Anya seeks extra-human explanation.

The efforts of Delbo and Schaeffer to account for survival in some all-embracing manner do not have real parallels in Gerda Klein's Holocaust memoir, *All But My Life*. Thus the major self-effacing characteristic of *Anya* and *None of Us Will Return*, namely a discrepancy between action and interpretation, is absent from Klein. Another difference between Klein and the other texts is that she does not refer much either to unconscious life forces or to divine protection. Raised in a traditional Jewish home, Klein apparently retains her faith without making God responsible for her own or anyone's fate. In telling her survival story, Klein refers to a variety of factors which helped her and lets the evidence speak for itself.

A major concrete factor increasing Klein's survival chances is undoubtedly the training in weaving which she undergoes in Bolkenhain, her first camp, and the need of the Reich for skilled laborers. Klein acknowledges her status when this training saves her from hard labor in Märzdorf and she is suddenly restored to operating looms in Landeshut: "We now knew beyond doubt that we were valuable."[29] Because of this skill, she spends most of her time in deportation in a series of labor camps. Although there is sporadic violence from supervisors and periods of food scarcity and overwork, especially toward the end, in general the weavers are much better fed than inmates in ordinary concentration camps. Selections for gassing are not mentioned until Grünberg, the last camp. In all of Klein's camps, the inmates sleep in individual bunks, have access to real bathrooms, and work a day or night shift with some time off for rest. All of these conditions are non-existent in death camps, except for the highly privileged. Bolkenhain and Landeshut (her first and third camps) provide relatively humane conditions, while Märzdorf and Grünberg (her second and fourth camps) are the worst. As the camps are evacuated in 1945, Klein must face a death march which is among the worst experiences of the Holocaust.

Despite the decisive advantage of her work, Klein makes the sustaining memory of her family loom largest in importance among survival factors. In contradiction with statements acknowledging her new independence after deportation, Klein continues to return to her memory images of a united family and the idea of reunion after liberation despite near certainty that all have perished. Describing her parents' loving conversation the night before their separation, Klein attributes great significance to their example for her ensuing life. The commemoration resembles many works in which accounting for survival and honoring the dead become almost synonymous: "Their courage ignited within me a spark that continued to glow through the years of misery and defeat."[30] Although Klein tends to emphasize spiritual example and emotional support, she gives some importance to concrete assistance as well. She credits her father with making her wear her ski boots when she is deported in June. Klein believes the sturdy boots enabled her to survive a 1000-mile death march. "I wonder why Papa insisted; how could he possibly have known?"[31]

Klein's girlfriend Ilse, deported from their Silesian town of Bielitz, Poland, at the same time as Klein, saves Klein's life twice in the memoir, once in Märzdorf when Klein is close to death from penal work and again on the death march, when Ilse's fear prevents Klein from trying to escape. Ilse is clearly very important to Klein, and her death represents a great loss, but she has a subordinate role in the narrative compared to the images of Klein's family.

The compromising aspect of working in German war factories seems to trouble Klein less than surviving her entire family. She emphasizes the difficulty of the work and the achievement of learning how to operate looms and spinning machines. In a relatively short time, Klein says, the inmate workers of Bolkenhain are tending four looms, more than experts after a lifetime of experience. The work involves continuous running, deafens the ears because of the noise, and produces severe eyestrain. "How I worked those first weeks I will never know. My fingers worked without conscious direction. I worked mechanically and watched the movement of the clock's hands."[32] While Klein at first attributes her ability to work to automatic, unconscious movements (comparable to Delbo's inexplicable strength and Anya's "something"), she later admits to an awareness of achievement: "In a way I began to like my work, I found a new security in it, for the intricate process of weaving gave me a sense of satisfaction and accomplishment."[33] In a similar way in other camps, her attitude toward work often raises her above the condition of complete enslavement, although the work is for the enemy.

However important this work may be, Klein's most effective shield against her oppressors is her imagination, which provides her with a link to her family and other people. This strategy provides her with a form of covert resistance which works in varying conditions. The most frequent content of her mental images is her brother and parents, but they take other shapes as well. A picture of her Russian grandfather, sent in a letter, reminds her of his miraculous survival: sentenced unjustly to life imprisonment as an old man, he was released by the Bolsheviks and returned home to find all his sons had survived the war. The story sustains Gerda through the trauma of a loom accident. On other occasions, Gerda is able to extend her imaginative faculty into a strategy for group resistance. In Bolkenhain, she writes skits which she and other girls perform for the others, and they are powerfully effective against fear and suffering. Here Klein becomes, figuratively and literally, self-dramatizing. "I know that that was the greatest thing I have done in my life."[34] Klein's capacity to use her imagination is indirectly related to survival through the sustaining of hope. It is also an instrument of private or covert resistance, a way of defeating Nazi aims by maintaining an inner world independent of outward oppression.

All But My Life reveals a mixture of self-effacing and self-dramatizing elements and moments. Essentially it is a survival story with some elements of the resistance narrative. Both Klein's maturing process and the fluctuating level of danger in the environment influence the type of characterization which she creates. In the early episodes, the memoir conveys the quick growing up of a shy girl into an assertive woman under the constraint of threatening events. In addition, it suggests the multiplicity of conditions to be found in camps other than death camps. The protagonist presents herself in three main stages of self-portrayal, which may be labelled self-effacing survival confrontations, self-dramatizing confrontations, and self-dramatizing daydreams in conflict with reality.

At the beginning of the German invasion of her Silesian town of Bielitz, Poland, Gerda Klein is a timid, fifteen-year-old schoolgirl from a religious, sheltering family. During this early period, she deals successfully with Gestapo danger three times, and yet she portrays herself each time as frightened and nearly helpless. Significantly, the guilt of possibly endangering her parents contributes to the negative value she places on her actions. She warns her father's business associate to hide from the Gestapo, which is searching for him, but fears being given away by the man's secretary. Arrested for carrying an English grammar book, she faces the examining officer mute with fear and is unexpectedly released. Later she lies to an official who demands her father, who is hiding in a closet in their ghetto room. Here she deals repeatedly with events for which nothing has prepared anyone, much less a sheltered teenaged girl.

The next section of the memoir, which describes Gerda's imprisonment in a transit camp (Sosnowitz), contains the most self-dramatizing confrontations. Completely separated from her family and not yet in mortal danger, neither the fear of harming her family nor the struggle to survive seem overriding issues. In

Sosnowitz, she requests and obtains a permit from the Commander to visit the parents of Abek Feigenblatt (her friend/suitor). The confrontation is a new kind of encounter with an official for Gerda Klein: she initiates the meeting, masters a confrontation with a powerful but corrupt Jewish official, and does this not for survival but only to get a permit to pay a social visit.

Klein dramatizes in detail how she succeeds in taking control of the encounter. She enters the official's office through a private entrance instead of joining a crowd trying to bribe a guard outside. She manages to suggest her superiority to the other Jews there, to conceal her own fear, and to exploit the man's vulnerability of not knowing German and Polish as well as she. The signals of her victory are the permit he gives her, the rebuke he silently accepts for his treatment of the other people, and the fact that he remains standing as she leaves, "an honor that he probably accorded no one else but the SS."[35] This scene contrasts with survivor-official confrontations in Delbo and Schaeffer in two important ways: The protagonist here dramatizes herself as the victor of a verbal contest in which the fact of winning dignity is more important than any survival benefits, and she takes maximum responsibility for her actions. Klein wonders where she is getting her lines, feeling like an actress acting a new role. She discovers a new, aggressive self that is as real as her old, timid self and finally acknowledges the new role and strength as her own.

I was thoroughly shaken. I hardly knew myself. I had never spoken like that. I had never felt like that. I was different in a thousand ways from yesterday. But the knowledge that such strength was within me gave me the courage to go on.[36]

In a development related to the above incident, Klein again maximizes a moment of triumph over a camp official. Because of a strict adherence to personal ethical principles, she rejects an offer which seems useful to her survival: Abek Feigenblatt's family wants her to live with them. She decides to reject this offer to avoid the obligation of marrying Abek, whom she does not love. Her second thoughts come too late. Yet while boarding the train to leave Sosnowitz, a guard brings her a letter from the Commander of the transit camp (from whom she had won the permit described above). He, too, wants her to stay in Sosnowitz.

With an impulsive gesture I tore the Commander's unopened envelope into shreds and let them drop out the window. I enjoyed seeing the baffled expression on the Militz man's face. I smiled in triumph. It was wonderful to feel so important.[37]

Klein dramatizes her negative answer, maximizing her defiance of a collaborator, as well as, in a hidden way, her rejection of an undesired marriage bond. The disparity between her rigorous moral principles, which oblige her to marry the son of benefactors even in an extreme situation, and the obvious collaboration of the Jewish Commander with the SS, is ironic. Her conservative ethics seem to be unaffected by the extraordinary prevailing conditions. Klein is not aware of the danger ahead; on the trip she bets with a friend that the war will last six months. In view of later events, the moment of victory is doubly ironic. When she faces the reality of deportation later, Gerda will regret not staying in Sosnowitz, then will learn that everyone in Sosnowitz has been deported to Auschwitz. Her rejection of both Abek and the Commander's offer is a personal victory based on partial information, later confirmed by luck.

Following transfer to Bolkenhain, a German labor camp, Gerda's relations with the Nazis change again. Resistance confrontations with Nazis become undesirable and often too dangerous. At Bolkenhain and Landeshut, the SS and functionaries are relatively harmless for the most part. However, in Grünberg and during the evacuation march, Klein experiences much more brutality, both personally and vicariously. Her aggressive impulses are now expressed silently in mental images while, overtly, she must express obedience and indifference. On her first morning in Grünberg, she watches the vicious director attack the face of a girl in the shower with his signet-ringed fingers. Paralyzed with "horror and rage," she imagines killing the man, enjoying "the sight of his blood," and if attacked herself, striking back without regard for safety.[38] However, when she is beaten only five pages later in a collective punishment, she is quite demoralized (see discussion, page 5). The combination of dreams of revenge and the reality of obedience also recur in condensed form during the death march of the evacuated inmates.

I had dreams about stealing a gun from an SS man during the night and shooting them all. But those were only dreams—I didn't even know how to fire a gun. Why did we march? Why did we let them slaughter us? . . . What difference would it have made if they had killed some of us?[39]

Although the revenge fantasies are compelling, Klein remembers her promise to her family to be strong and her responsibility to survive in case they do. Her actions remain consistent with the goal of survival rather than with her revenge dreams.

Although *All But My Life* is essentially a survival narrative, the author is at times interested in showing moments of dramatic resistance as well as a more covert resistance based on fantasy. Klein's relegating of most self-dramatizing moments in the camps to fantasy is a feature which increases her credibility. Because of the variety of situations, the nature of the labor camps and factories described, and the tendency to let evidence speak for itself, the characterization is a mix of self-effacing and self-dramatizing elements. As a result, Holocaust suffering appears much less severe than in Delbo and somewhat less than in Schaeffer.

Self-dramatizing Resistance Mode

We now turn to a group of Holocaust works in which the balance of attention shifts away from survival and toward resistance. Resisting Nazis tends to place the protagonist in dangerous confrontations which she wins either physically or morally. While the self-effacing protagonist may also demonstrate bravery in confronting the enemy, her reasons are primarily for survival and not mostly self-idealization or moral opposition. The self-dramatizing survivor portrays herself most consistently in a fighter role against Nazi aims. Since resistance implies the role of the individual will, personal accountability is much less of an issue than in those texts where survival is the main thing to be explained. The issue of survival tends to diminish in importance without disappearing; it remains the object of an intense struggle, but a different concern has become primary in the telling of the story.

The popular imagination has associated Holocaust resistance with armed resistance, which occurred at certain times and places, such as the Warsaw Ghetto Uprising, the burning down of Treblinka and Sobibor, and the blowing up of the Auschwitz crematoria. These were desperate acts by victims of Nazism who had lost a reasonable hope for survival and wanted to give meaning to their deaths. However, there are many other ways in which inmates could express resistance to total domination. Holocaust narratives feature a wide range of resistance actions, both overt and covert. Overt resistance could include any kind of confrontation, symbolic or physical, which the enemy could see. This might include the showing of symbols of opposition, such as objects, music, or facial expressions; verbal combat; threats of violence; and violence. Covert resistance includes personal thoughts, secret communications between inmates, and any other form of opposition to Nazi aims which remains hidden.

Although both hidden and open types of resistance occur in camp literature, the degree of danger attached to overt confrontation of Nazis in ghettos and camps is so great that its appearance in a memoir needs more explanation than the more expected covert resistance. Comments in many survivor documents stress that, in a camp, any kind of talking back, even an expression showing minor defiance, could be fatal. It was the norm for inmates to wear a mask of indifference, above all to be inconspicuous. On the other hand, conditions were unpredictable; sometimes a prisoner could confront an SS officer or supervisor without undue danger, for example, with a request for a different work assignment. Inmates working in protected positions such as registering new arrivals, recording deaths, or playing in the orchestra, had closer contact with the SS and thus different kinds of encounters with them. Whatever the actual conditions of the ghettos and camps, the act of writing about the experience often gives the survivor an opportunity to maximize moments of defiance in order to express long suppressed anger. This function of the memoir is as valid as that of expressing the guilt and sadness of survival, but it sometimes presents difficulties in disentangling the writer's emotional venting from the actual possibilities existing during the period of persecution.

The concepts of survival and resistance, which are central in any discussion of Holocaust literature, are useful for schematizing literary phenomena but also have their limitations. Survival could be seen as a form of resistance since it implies a frustration of Nazi aims, generally involves struggle and risk, and can be seen as a kind of victory over the Holocaust. But many Holocaust narratives do not give survival the same value as other forms of resistance. Although the Holocaust may have caused survival to acquire greater intrinsic value than before, other more traditional views have dominated many memoirs. In addition, the most common view of resistance continues to see it in terms of armed struggle and to dismiss survival as *mere* survival.

The balance between survival and resistance goals and the strategies for giving literary expression to them depend on a number of factors, including the degree of danger to which the survivor character is exposed. The protagonists of resistance narratives tend to be privileged prisoners who can afford to risk survival in expressing resistance, for whom survival is not *the* overwhelming struggle. The privileged position of Fania Fénelon is the result of her musical talents and acceptance into the Birkenau orchestra. As a high-status member of this elite group, she is protected from the fatal conditions of the death camp as long as the orchestra remains in favor with the SS. In her position as an SS entertainer, she comes into relatively close contact with these officials with far greater safety than an ordinary inmate. Her position makes it possible for her to take certain risks to demonstrate her resistance. Judith Dribben's special assets include an "Aryan" appearance in combination with skill in languages, role playing, and partisan resistance activities. She is able to maintain a disguise as a non-Jewish Russian spy in prison and in Birkenau and thus to avoid the worst treatment which is reserved for Jews. She obtains the protection of the camp resistance organization and manages to find privileged positions as translator and clerk.

In Livia Bitton Jackson's *Elli*, protected status is much less important than other factors. The protagonist's intuitive knowledge of the hidden truth about Nazi deceptions and a self-portrayal which implies divine protection constitute the key elements of her privilege. The teenaged protagonist and her mother spend significant amounts of time in ordinary outdoor labor details, and when they manage to find favored factory work, the protected status does not change the narrator's self characterization much. A memoir such as *Elli* makes a useful comparison to the books by Dribben and Fénelon because it guards against oversimplifying explanations of character type.

A common feature of the characters in the self-dramatizing mode is that they all express overt (visible) opposition to the enemy. Thus, in contrast to the problem of locating the cause of survival in the self-effacing mode, resistance aims maximize the role of personal initiative in these works. Judith Dribben volunteers as a partisan soon after the Nazi invasion of her town, Lvov, and consistently volunteers for difficult assignments. Fénelon takes chances several times to express her opposition by making use of opportune moments. Fénelon acts in opposition not only to the Nazis but also to the desires for security of her peers in the Birkenau orchestra and to her own more hidden survival interests. Elli's most remarkable action is her physically pushing away an SS woman who is attacking her mother, although such an action would normally lead to death.

Playing for Time is a fictionalized memoir in which Fania Fénelon describes her experiences in Birkenau between January and November, 1944, and in Bergen-Belsen from November, 1944 to April 15, 1945. Fénelon, a half-Jewish night club singer, is arrested for assisting the French Resistance and is deported to Birkenau. Shortly after her initiation to the camp, she passes a singing audition before *Lagerführerin* Maria Mandel and thus gains admission into the women's orchestra in Birkenau. This group of forty-seven inmates from many countries has the job of entertaining the SS and playing daily marches for the ordinary prisoners leaving the camp for work. Their privileged position in the camp gives them indoor work, good clothing and living quarters, and a reprieve from selections, but no reprieve from the rations or the fear of a sudden end to their status.

Since the SS have a personal interest in keeping the orchestra alive, the members are not engaged in the overwhelming struggle for survival of the ordinary inmates. The memoir has a different focus: it highlights the efforts of Fénelon to express defiance against the SS and their *kapo*. Rather than any grand actions, resistance in *Playing for Time* consists of a series of small gestures which are important in the setting and are highlighted through the dramatic tension of the situation. In an early episode, for example, Fania Fénelon describes her revulsion and paralysis which nearly prevent her from singing for the SS. "I felt as though I were living through one of those nightmares in which you want to cry out and can't."[40] However, she masters herself enough to sing, after which she defies *Lagerführer* Kramer in a small way. When he asks her if any supplies are needed, she expresses her need for pencils for her copyists by handing him the one marked "Made in England," saying, "this." He does nothing to show he understands the subtle provocation, but afterwards the other orchestra members become outraged when they learn what she has done. Their fear dramatizes the risk which she has taken. Her reply is a self-dramatizing show of bravado which minimizes her fear of the gas chamber, a concern which is far greater at other times. "We'll end up there sooner or later in any case, and at least we'll have shown them we don't give a damn about them. . . . If we're going to be gassed, we might as well go smiling."[41] The symbolic gesture is fairly safe because Kramer lacks the intelligence to understand, as one of the inmates points out. Fénelon's egocentric pose is a way of asserting the value of small acts of resistance despite her outward collaboration.

Fénelon takes a bigger risk with "Graf Bobby," an SS officer who nonchalantly separates the new arrivals to be gassed from those who enter the camps. He asks her a provocative question based upon the Nazis' poorly concealed secret about the gas chambers: Why did so few of the new Hungarian Jewish arrivals volunteer when he asked for musicians? Perhaps, he suggests, when they get to the camp to which the SS is sending them, they may volunteer after all. Fénelon answers ambiguously that they may lose their fear. The officer then asks her, if she were in their place and they were in hers, would she send her enemies where they send theirs? She dares to answer that she certainly would but would not send women, children, or old people.[42] He appreciates her wit enough to compliment her on her answer.

The other players shout invective at her for taking risks with their lives. For her, however, it is a chance to verbally reassert her dignity instead of always trying to please her oppressors.

In addition to these verbal barbs, Fénelon's position in the orchestra gives her the opportunity to exploit music as covert symbolic resistance. She orchestrates music by forbidden Jewish composers and other music with special significance to the orchestra members, such as the first movement of Beethoven's Fifth Symphony, the signature tune of the Free French broadcasts on the BBC. The significance of the music remains unknown to the SS, a deception which lifts the morale of the players.

While Fénelon is the main originator of resistance acts in the memoir, she is not the only one. Marta, a German political prisoner in the orchestra, defies a female SS warden by means of a facial expression. The big, disgusted Nazi gives Marta a kick for doing a poor job of scrubbing the floor and proceeds to demonstrate her own skill. It is an amazing sight and a stunning role reversal: the feared SS woman on her hands and knees, while the seventeen-year-old prisoner stands erect, "observing the SS woman at her feet with utter insolence."[43] The warden, formerly a maid in Marta's house, arrogantly tells Marta, "That's how you wash a floor, now you know!" Marta's contemptuous answer, "Ja, Frau Aufseherin!" elicits the desperate swallowing of Alma, the *kapo*, because confronting the SS was absolutely against the rules.[44]

The unusual role reversal and Marta's gesture of defiance have lasting collective benefits. Although it is a small act of rebellion, it enters the group's heroic mythology, becoming the basis for distracting conversations. Fénelon's style maximizes the effects of such small acts, but the importance to inmates of small acts of assistance or kindness is often mentioned in the documentation on the camps, and the same seems true for resistance acts.

Since survival is an important personal and collective goal in *Playing for Time*, most of Fénelon's rebellion and anger must be concealed beneath a mask of indifference. Her rage emerges narratively in sarcastic and vivid descriptions of the SS and prisoner officials. Commandant Kramer's sensitivity to music despite his cruelty to women prisoners elicits one of her bitterest attacks, as she describes the "tears as precious as pearls" which he allowed "to roll down his carefully shaven cheeks" and compares the relief he gets from music to masturbation.[45] Here Fénelon clearly uses the memoir as a belated weapon against one of the chief Auschwitz torturers.

Fénelon's relations to Alma Rosé, the German-Jewish conductor, constitute a tenuous balance between obedience and resistance. She withholds her approval for Alma's identification with the Germans and her treatment of the players (Fénelon makes her responsible for the miserable food rations which they receive, identical to the ordinary inmates). However, neither does she influence Alma's behavior much nor complain much directly to her. Alma is unlikely to punish her for small acts of defiance, such as pronouncing the German "ch" incorrectly, because Fania is too valuable to the orchestra to lose.

While most of Fénelon's resistance gestures are modest during imprisonment, she uses an effective threat of violence once against a *kapo*, namely against the ineffective and unpopular Ukrainian pianist who replaces Alma Rosé after the latter dies. This is the only instance where there is a clear danger to a life in the orchestra. Fénelon prevents Sonia from taking Florette, one of her friends, to the SS as punishment for stealing a few potatoes. She threatens to suffocate Sonia in bed if she does not let the girl go. Sonia believes the seriousness of the threat and lets her go.

Resistance possibilities diminish in the Bergen-Belsen camp, to which Fania Fénelon and the other orchestra members are transferred as the Russian troops advance. In this section, the status of the orchestra members reduces to that of the ordinary inmates. Some become workers in a cellophane factory, while the rest must clear trees. As the war moves to its conclusion, starvation, disease, and death take over. On April 15, 1945, as Fénelon lies near death with typhus, the British liberate the camp hours before the SS plan to shoot all the remaining inmates. Here the changing environment with the loss of privilege and the role of chance make the characterization much less self-dramatizing. Only following liberation, in an incident placed at the beginning of the memoir, does Fénelon manage the theatrical gesture of singing the *Marseillaise* into a BBC microphone despite illness and a weight of only sixty-two pounds. The memoir thus begins with the twin images of Fénelon as an ordinary sick, skeletal prisoner and as a quite unique singer.

A second example of the self-dramatizing resistance protagonist is found in Judith Strick Dribben's fictionalized memoir, *A Girl Called Judith Strick*. Dribben presents herself as a consistently strong, aggressive fighter of Nazis and Nazism by emphasizing her personal victories in numerous verbal and violent battles. Dribben quickly establishes her unusual readiness to fight the Nazi occupiers: a university graduate in law and administration from Lvov, Poland, she looks for work with Germans in her city that will allow her "to face the enemy, penetrate army units, to study what was going on there."[46] She exploits her job of cleaning for the German police by secretly examining their files, initiating her own training as a spy. Soon thereafter she joins her friend Peter's underground group and remains an active Polish partisan for sixteen months (June, 1941 to October, 1942), then remains associated with resistance members during her seventeen months in Birkenau and Hirtenberg. Her warrior role outlasts her liberation, as she fights briefly with the Russian Army, then, following emigration to Palestine, joins the Irgun to fight Arabs. Later she becomes a captain and the first woman intelligence officer in the Israeli Army.

Dribben's unusual aptitudes and experiences are the basis for an account which maximizes her control over her fate during the Holocaust. A highly significant factor in her ability to survive is her non-Jewish appearance, but she de-emphasizes this fact. After mentioning it twice briefly at the start of the German occupation of Lvov, Dribben does not refer to it again. Yet her "Aryan" appearance is essential for her to maintain a series of non-Jewish disguises, including that of partisan disguised as seductress or domestic maid, stranded Frenchwoman, and Russian spy. To emphasize this would reduce the impression of Dribben's control over her survival and resistance efforts. Less hidden, and more within her control, is a knowledge of six languages. Other accidental gifts include general intelligence and a vivid imagination, an extraordinary aptitude for military strategy (especially considering her gender), and a good deal of personal aggression and confidence.

Dribben's attitude toward her own survival fluctuates, but in general she presents a profile of resistance which seems to scorn survival as a goal. Her most self-dramatizing confrontations occur during her year in Polish prisons, where she deceives her captors by inventing a series of identities and battling them verbally during months of interrogation. She responds more than once to severe beatings by shouting insults at them.

"I'll die with honor, don't worry, but you'll be mounted on the gallows, together with the whole rotten bunch, after you get knocked out." I was interrupted by another blow on my face. "You swine!" I lost my control. "Wait, the day will come when you'll dance with Hitler in the air—"
"Shut up, shut up!" the officer screamed. "We have means of breaking you down. We'll show you."
"Don't be an idiot," I said, suddenly quiet. "You can kill me but I won't be a traitor." He understood it this time and calmed down.[47]

Dribben claims not only the dignity of verbally fighting back but also the power to stop the attacks. Her fearlessness is difficult to believe, even though she supplies rationalizations. Her interrogators believe they may still get valuable information from her, since she has persuaded them that she is a Russian spy. Major von Korab, her senior interrogator, tells her that when his department loses interest in her she will face a firing squad. She believes she can keep their interest, since her stories hold them spellbound. As a result, she can reject their offer of freedom in exchange for collaboration with such flamboyant remarks as: "I acted against the German army and I want to be brought before a court-martial. I am sick and tired of the Gestapo imbeciles. Give me a court-martial!"[48]

Dribben's typical dismissal of survival as a chief concern during these prison interrogations seems bolstered by some real advantages of safety. Her role as partisan demonstrably protects her several times from death. Although the partisan role seems to be more dangerous than hiding or awaiting deportation, Dribben's personal story suggests the opposite: while soldiers discover the hiding place of her mother and brother on a farm and kill them, she and other partisans experience liberation (but not her fiancé). In Birkenau, her status as political prisoner is an even clearer advantage over the ordinary prisoner, since the Gestapo gives her a privileged clerk job upon entry and spares her the total shaving for Jewish women. Although her status declines later, she benefits from an easy adjustment period and protection from the camp underground. The great advantages of non-Jews over Jews in the camps is well documented. Thus, for Dribben, survival is in part a by-product of being a partisan, a role defined by courting danger.

Dribben conceives of her position as privileged and feels compelled to justify to herself her protection from the general Jewish fate. This justification is, not surprisingly, "fighting back," which she sees in rational militant terms, a matter of individual control:

I asked myself the question: How come that you escaped from your people and their fate? How can you enjoy a certain degree of freedom while they are condemned to death? But what would I prove by being another victim of the Nazi regime? What would I accomplish by waiting helplessly for the day of my extermination? No, I preferred to be a partisan and fight back.[49]

Dribben presents the choices of the Jews reductively as waiting for extermination or fighting back. She asserts that for long stretches of time, she suppresses not only any guilt feelings but all memory of her true identity. What she also suppresses, apparently, is the awareness that the luck of her appearance and abilities separates her from the victimization afflicting most other Jews.[50]

Dribben's division of the 340 pages of the memoir into four unequal sections contributes to her self-dramatizing style. The three sections dealing with the period of the war and Holocaust cover 1) Dribben's resistance activities from June, 1941 to October, 1942; 2) her one year of imprisonment; 3) and her one and one-half years in concentration camps. The second period offers the greatest opportunities for self-dramatization due to her outwitting her prison captors, but its actual duration is the shortest time. It has the largest number of pages, ninety-one, a way of emphasizing Dribben's strongest moments. Her sixteen months as a free partisan receive eighty pages, while her eighteen months as a camp inmate are covered in the shortest section, sixty-four pages. By making Dribben's dramatic verbal confrontations with Gestapo interrogators dominate the memoir, while restricting her longer period of greater suffering to a shorter section, Dribben emphasizes the possibilities of winning and avoiding victimization. She further stresses the positive outcome by adding ninety-seven pages on her unusual military role in the struggle for the Jewish state.

The concentration camp section of the memoir is written more objectively. It adds credibility to the whole memoir because it describes conditions in Birkenau confirmed by other survivor texts. Dribben enters in the political prisoner category and receives the job of interpreter for the Political Department. Although she is able to use the position to give covert messages of resistance to new Russian-speaking arrivals, her status changes when she contracts typhus. Often fatal in the death camps, typhus does not kill her because her physician friends "organize" an injection for her. Having lost her favored position in the Political Department, she then must endure the most brutal outdoor work of the camp in one of the worst work groups. This consists of filling wagons with stones and pushing them along rails over a hill. The work is accompanied by floggings for minor mistakes or less, sporadic attacks by the SS dogs, and freezing weather. In this part, Dribben does not hide the suffering but still manages to suggest transcendence through her thoughts.

No hope. No courage. No spirit of friendship. Nothing. Every prisoner cared for herself. If someone was struck, you were grateful it was not you. Were we defeated? . . . We could not die; we wanted to live, just to live—this thought filled me completely, until I no longer felt the cold and the frosty wind.[51]

In addition to the reality of suffering, Dribben retains her customary stoicism by filling her mind with the thought of survival, even in this murderous setting. She continues her tough image following this passage, claiming the ability to maintain a positive attitude from getting clean clothes and seeing her block leader in forced gymnastics.

After surviving two difficult battles with illness, she is transferred to Hirtenberg, a satellite of Mauthausen in Germany. Here she works as a camp recorder and is able to assist sabotage indirectly in the camp ammunition factory by protecting the identity of the workers. She exploits her position and restores her self-dramatizing characterization as outwitter of the SS. The section ends with a short evacuation march, from which she and others are able to escape due to the confusion and drunkenness of the SS.

Dribben represents one Israeli view of the Holocaust. Her superhero approach is not duplicated by Livia E. Bitton Jackson, a Hungarian-born American-Israeli, living in Israel since 1977.[52] She patterns her self-portrayal as a composite of suffering and combat within a framework of traditional religious values. Elli's thirteen-year-old consciousness provides the perspective on her family's deportation experience as told by the adult survivor. Unlike Dribben and Fénelon, Jackson does not use privileged camp status as a vantage point from which to demonstrate resistance, even though Elli and her mother find favored jobs in an Augsburg factory for several months. Neither does Elli's blond hair take up any space after it initially saves her and her mother from Mengele's selection on the Auschwitz railroad ramp (he tells her to pretend to be sixteen).

Jackson's religious perspective creates a survival story somewhat similar to Schaeffer's *Anya*, but also different. Like the latter, she is continually acting to save family members and often evoking the role of a divine agency. In this memoir the narrator sometimes acknowledges unexpected survivals with the words "miracle" and "thank God." Elli, her mother, and other women at times endure difficult ordeals by resorting to traditional religious observance. But by not emphasizing the problem of accounting for survival and by implicitly crediting successful actions to her own initiative, Jackson takes more responsibility for her actions than Anya. The memoir also has more uniformity of tone than the novel; in *Anya* the protagonist in the epilogue reflects much more of the physical and mental torments of survival than one finds in *Elli*. The risks which she takes in defiance of Auschwitz rules (she is there twice in addition to three other camps) result in dramatic personal victories, although these risks grow directly out of her strong need to protect her mother. This is particularly true in the Birkenau episode in which Elli shoves an SS woman against a wall because the officer has been twisting the paralyzed arm of Elli's sick mother. The vicious beating which Elli gets in retaliation might have been described as one more Holocaust horror, but it becomes something else in Jackson's hands. Once the painful details of punches, kicks, blood, and numbness have been recorded, the narrator's consciousness focusses on her miraculous survival despite attacking an SS officer, "the gravest possible form of sabotage."[53] Because Jackson describes this event as a victory without denying her pain or the need from which it springs, she employs a self-dramatizing strategy with considerable persuasiveness.

In addition to physical defense, Jackson asserts the positive value of physical suffering in an unusual manner as an element in her self-dramatizing portrait. Elli's body registers loss and tragedy with severe and recurrent abdominal pains and nausea, but instead of making it a sign of victimization, Jackson converts this pain into a measure of her superior awareness of events. Elli's foreknowledge of her father's death while they are still at home in Somorja, Hungary, stems from her interpretation of a dream of her father's impending fate and her subsequent abdominal pain. When her father is deported, she describes her hysterical sobs as an expression of knowledge as well as of grief.

All the self-delusions of the ghetto suddenly melted away. The delusions which had lulled me into a false sense of security and had made the gnawing subside were suddenly part of the cloud of dust which swallowed the last sights of my father.[54]

Thus Elli sets herself apart from the other people who cling to illusory hopes that their fate will not be too harsh. Only her Aunt Szerén also expresses real horror at the impending deportation by hurling her teacups at the walls. Elli screams her awareness that they will never see each other again as her aunt is selected for death on the Auschwitz ramp. More practical results stem from the "horrible certainty" at Waldlager Camp that the skeletal robot standing before her and her mother is her brother, Bubi. Only after recognition has been established can they share their bread with him, thus slowly metamorphosing him from a *Muslim* back into a human being.[55] Although Jackson and her mother have been told that they are about to see Bubi, Jackson stresses the importance of her ability to sense that he is there, even when her mother does not.

By allowing intuitive awareness and undenied pain to stand for a divine and human presence at Auschwitz, Jackson creates a unique Holocaust resistance narrative. She uses the memoir to document her superiority over her fate by means of faith and a resistance of awareness and action. What links her with the other self-dramatizing heroines is not privilege or status, but rather power, which in her case is presented with a source different from the camp hierarchy. The memoir presents camp status as helpful at times but undependable, as Bubi's story illustrates: from a highly privileged position as translator for the Auschwitz SS, he sinks to the abyss described above in Waldlager. Elli and her mother's factory work in Augsburg is protected from starvation, beatings, and selections but is preceded and followed by grimmer episodes at Auschwitz and Plaszow.

Whereas Elli's special awareness of events appears to link her with the shelter of extra-human power, Fénelon is protected by her position in the orchestra and Dribben by her partisan role and non-Jewish disguise. These self-dramatizing survivors all claim more consistent privilege, power, and victory than the self-effacing survivors. The privileges and status of Anya in Schaeffer's novel and Klein in her memoir are lesser and more temporary.

However, the connection posed between privilege and resistance is not a simple one. When one examines some other Holocaust narratives dealing with privileged prisoners, one does not always find the connection between high status and self-dramatization. For example, Jenny Spritzer's memoir *Ich war Nr. 10291* (*I Was Number 10291*) delineates the author's experiences as a clerk in the Birkenau Political Department with great objectivity and restraint.[56] Although she works in an elite position in close proximity to SS officers, this Dutch Jewish woman only rarely describes personal acts of defiance against them and refrains from celebrating these acts. She emphasizes the secretaries' fear of the SS officers, warranted not only by the fate from which they have been rescued, but also by the screams of tortured prisoners which penetrate the office walls from an adjacent interrogation room.

Another fictionalized memoir which does not dramatize individual resistance as one might expect is Vladka Meed's *On Both Sides of the Wall*.[57] The author, an "Aryan"-looking Polish Jew, tells of her experiences as a courier for the Jewish Resistance Organization of the Warsaw Ghetto. Her work of smuggling weapons into the ghetto and bringing messages and children out of it is intrinsically risky and heroic. However, Meed embeds her personal story into the larger tale of many interdependent underground fighters and the struggle of the Jewish Ghetto Uprising. She neither isolates her courage from that of others nor conceals their constant fears and sense of desperation at the great difficulties: lack of support from the Polish Underground, lack of arms, betrayals, etc.

These Holocaust memoirs suggest that neither privileged status in a death camp nor acting in a resistance organization fully explain the choice of a self-dramatizing character. Some Holocaust memoirs choose to emphasize a collective portrait while others focus more attention on the individual survivor. The group portrait naturally tends towards de-emphasizing the importance of the individual survivor and acknowledges the historical fact of mass or collective persecution more directly. Among the self-effacing texts discussed, one stands out by far as the most collective in focus and strategy. This memoir is Delbo's *None of Us Will Return*. An appropriate question is whether Delbo's memoir has anything in common with those by Jenny Spritzer and Vladka Meed, other than subordinance of individual to collective fate. Delbo's memoir was written shortly after her liberation and then published twenty years later in 1965; Delbo wanted to judge the truth of her writing over this period of time before showing it to the public.[58] Vladka Meed's book was first published in 1948; Spritzer's appeared in 1946. These publication dates are much earlier than those of Judith Dribben (whose memoir first appeared in 1969 as *And Some Shall Live)* or Fénelon's *Playing For Time* (1976), or Jackson's *Elli* (1980). From this small group of texts it appears that memoirs written within a few years of the events described are more likely to be oriented toward a group portrait and more likely to follow a soberly documentary strategy than a self-dramatizing pattern. The mixed or intermediate type of narrative found in Klein's *All But My Life* was published in 1957, still relatively early. However, such a novel as *Anya*, a self-effacing survival story, was published quite late: 1974. It may be that historical fiction is more variable in terms of the relationship between date and type than autobiographical works. Sidra Ezrahi has commented that a number of survivors have written Holocaust memoirs or histories before writing Holocaust fiction, "as if to establish the historicity of the subject before admitting it to the imagination."[59] There may also be a stronger impulse toward "objective" and collective memoirs while the memories are still fresh and a turning toward more imaginative, dramatic memoirs after more years have passed.

Holocaust narratives describe a variety of survivor types which embody much more than victimization or heroism. The choice of an individual or collective focus and the stance of objective detachment or emotional involvement have a strong impact on the resulting narrative. Camp conditions and work assignments can have a significant impact, but even when they are quite similar from one text to another, the narrator's voice may be strongly colored by different motives for writing: bearing witness, seeking revenge, mourning and expressing attachments to the dead, asking for the public's understanding, and seeking to prevent other Holocausts. The variety is more restricted than in the whole corpus of autobiographies or memoirs but also greater than some Holocaust critics have suspected.

These Holocaust narratives with their variety of character types have a message for those who study the writings of women. The theories produced by feminist criticism depend upon the texts selected, and these are rarely about extreme situations. For example, in Estelle Jelinek's "Women's Autobiography and the Male Tradition," she asserts that while men usually write self-confident, self-idealizing autobiographies, women write in a self-effacing style and their aim is often "to convince readers of their self-worth, to clarify, to affirm, and to authenticate their self-image."[60] This gender distinction is not as valid for women's Holocaust memoirs, since Dribben, Fénelon, and often Jackson exemplify the "male" self-aggrandizing style. The presence of women in Holocaust resistance roles which survivor authors sometimes magnify in their narratives is a factor which a general theory such as Jelinek's and many others need to take into account.

Furthermore, the distinction which Jelinek draws between seeking affirmation and understanding and the projecting of self-idealizing images may not hold for women's Holocaust memoirs. Internal evidence often refers to the use of small resistance gestures, magnified in order to deny one's compliance in the oppression. The need to assert resistance actions by self-dramatizing memoirists often stems from the need to replace the victim or collaborator image of Holocaust Jews with a stronger image. Fénelon alludes to this need when she refers to the negative image of the Birkenau orchestra in other memoirs, and when she describes her self disgust at singing for the SS. Dribben alludes only a few times to troubled feelings when faced with Jewish victims, but her self portrait is so uniformly militant and tough that it demands admiration at the expense of believability. One assumes that Dribben is also fighting the "like sheep to the slaughter" charge that weighs on many Holocaust survivors. Given this motive, the self-aggrandizing image appears to be linked in these texts to a justification of self.

Notes

1. Barbara Foley, "Fact, Fiction, Fascism: Testimony and Mimesis in Holocaust Narratives," *Comparative Literature* 34, no. 4 (Fall, 1982): 330–60.

2. Terrence Des Pres, *The Survivor* (New York: Oxford University Press, 1976), p. 7.

3. Sidra Ezrahi, *By Words Alone: The Holocaust in Literature* (Chicago: The University of Chicago Press, 1980), p. 68.

4. Charlotte Delbo, *None of Us Will Return*, trans. John Githens (New York: Grove Press, 1968), p. 53.

5. Gerda Klein, *All But My Life* (New York: Hill and Wang, 1957), p. 174.

6. Ibid.

7. Susan Fromberg Schaeffer, *Anya* (New York: Avon Books, 1976), p. 320.

8. Ibid.

9. Delbo, p. 53.

10. Ibid., p. 104.

11. Fania Fénelon, *Playing for Time*, trans. Judith Landry (New York: Atheneum, 1976), pp. 10, 15.

12. Judith Dribben, *A Girl Called Judith Strick* (New York: Cowles Book Company, 1970), pp. 155–56.

13. Ibid., p. 157.

14. Ilse Aichinger, *Herod's Children*, trans. Cornelia Schaeffer (New York: Atheneum, 1963), p. 186.

15. Livia Bitton Jackson, *Elli* (New York: Times Books, 1980), p. 137.

16. Ibid.

17. Delbo, p. 93.

18. Ibid., p. 94.

19. Ibid., p. 72.

20. Ibid., p. 76.

21. Ibid., p. 128; Rosette C. Lamont, "Literature, the Exile's Agent of Survival: Alexander Solzhenitsyn and Charlotte Delbo," *Mosaic* 9, no. 1 (Fall, 1975): 6.

22. *None of Us Will Return* is the first volume of a trilogy which includes *Une connaissance inutile* (Paris: Editions de Minuit, 1970) and *Mesure de nos jours* (Paris: Editions de Minuit, 1971). The second two texts describe the author's experiences in labor camps other than Auschwitz.

23. Delbo, *None*, p. 13.

24. Schaeffer, p. 613.

25. Ibid., p. 244.

26. Ibid., p. 295.

27. Ibid.

28. Ibid., p. 218 ff.

29. Klein, p. 155.

30. Ibid., p. 86.

31. Ibid.

32. Ibid., p. 120.

33. Ibid., p. 133.

34. Ibid., p. 142.

35. Ibid., p. 100.

36. Ibid.

37. Ibid., pp. 111–12.

38. Ibid., p. 169.

39. Ibid., p. 192.

40. Fénelon, p. 93.

41. Ibid., p. 95 (partly my translation).

42. It is an answer clearly belonging to another era; at variance with the fact of brutal female SS, she appeals to the traditional exemption of women and children from war as a sign of superior civilization.

43. Fénelon, p. 138.

44. Ibid., p. 139. If it seems unlikely that an ex-maid in Marta's house is the warden of this scene, Olga Lengyel's remark refers to the incidence of similar events: "Frequently ironic situations resulted. One blocova, formerly maid-of-all-work, selected her erstwhile mistress as her personal servant. The latter brushed the shoes and mended the tatters of her ex-maid." *Five Chimneys: The Story of Auschwitz* (Chicago: Ziff-Davis, 1947).

45. Ibid., p. 92.

46. Dribben, p. 22.

47. Ibid., p. 143.

48. Ibid., p. 141.

49. Ibid., p. 74.

50. Edward Alexander, *The Resonance of Dust: Essays on Holocaust Literature and Jewish Fate* (Columbus: Ohio State University Press, 1979), p. 73.

51. Dribben, p. 202.

52. "Dr. Jackson, a professor of Judaic studies, moved from Germany to New York in 1951, and from New York to Israel in 1977." *New Yorker* 56 (May 19, 1980): 162.

53. Jackson, p. 138.

54. Ibid., pp. 41–42.

55. Ibid., p. 170.

56. Jenny Spritzer, *Ich war Nr. 10291*, 2nd ed. (Darmstadt: Verlag Darmstädter Blätter, 1980). (Originally published 1946.)

57. Vladka Meed, *On Both Sides of the Wall: Memoirs of the Warsaw Ghetto*, trans. M. Spiegel and S. Mead (Haifa: Ghetto Fighters House, 1972).

58. Joan Miriam Ringelheim, "The Unethical and the Unspeakable," *Simon Wiesenthal Center Annual* 1 (1984), p. 83.

59. Ezrahi, p. 22.

60. Estelle C. Jelinek, *Women's Autobiography* (Bloomington: Indiana University Press, 1980), p. 15.

III

INMATE RELATIONS IN
HOLOCAUST NARRATIVES

One of the curiosities of Holocaust memoirs is that the vast majority contain contradictory evidence about the predominance of selfishness over cooperation in the concentration and death camps. General statements about helping and comradeship stand side by side with assertions that the Nazi system set people against each other and that selfish responses were the norm. Some memoirs emphasize such egocentric responses as stealing food, rejecting communication with other inmates, or limiting concern to one's own suffering or safety. But sometimes the same accounts, or others, stress the comforting power of conversation, the saving of comrades' lives, or the pain of seeing others suffer. And the issue is complicated by the act of writing about the events from the distance of time. The survivor's present condition imprints itself on the retelling of the past: continued ties with the dead produce a sense of guilt and sadness but also a responsibility to bear witness to the unique events suffered in common. The survivor-author has frequently made the goal of bearing witness his or her reason to survive and often carries an implicit or explicit pact with the dead that whoever survives will assume the burden of speaking for the others. Only in this way will death not be absolute, as Terrence Des Pres has eloquently stated.[1] But this act of witnessing often conveys a multifaceted vision: the extraordinary otherness of the Holocaust, part of which is reflected in a self-centered battle for survival, multiplied many times and countered on the other hand by acts of decency and solidarity.

Each Holocaust memoirist must come up with a balance in writing about the tension between the egocentric and cooperative aspects of the experience, and this balance varies considerably. Egocentric survivor types often exist as secondary characters in the memoirs of "humane" survivors (those actively involved in communal sharing). Sometimes by separating him or herself clearly from such individuals, the narrator underscores his/her own ethical endurance. But since so many survivors still assert the primacy of egocentrism in the camps, one might justly ask whether the "communal" memoirist is hiding the reality about relationships and whether this reality could be uncovered in other texts.

If a survivor-author's memories of prisoner relations are tied to socially and psychologically determined roles, these roles are partly gender-based. No one has explored whether women and men write the same or differently about other camp inmates when they write their Holocaust memoirs, and this subject is the focus of this chapter. The issue of women's relationships with each other has occupied an important place in the work of feminist scholars during the past two decades. Psychoanalytical, literary, sociological, and political theorists have grappled with the obstacles and potentials in the way women relate or could relate with each other. Fundamental to this discourse is a critique of patriarchal society, particularly the institutions of marriage and family, which often isolate women from each other and promote loyalties to oppressive men. Literary critics, beginning with a critique of women portrayed as rivals for men in traditional texts, have sought other models in literary texts, including studies of friendship in which women of earlier times have found emotional sustenance unavailable to them in marriage. Others have studied the complex combinations of love and anger in mother-daughter relationships. They have uncovered a more varied tradition of female relationships than had been known previously.

An inquiry into the theme of women's relationships in concentration camp literature fills a void in the scholarship which has primarily concerned itself with conditions less fraught with danger and death. What happens to the sustaining possibilities of women's friendships in this literature? How is it different from those of men? Can we compare men and women fairly? Are men's and women's friendships equally valuable to camp inmates in extreme conditions?

To begin to answer these questions, it makes sense to inquire about possible gender differences in the writing of non-Holocaust autobiographical prose. Even if the Holocaust is radically different from "ordinary" subjects, the act of writing memoirs by survivors and non-survivors has basic resemblances. Estelle Jelinek's survey of men's and women's autobiographies indicates that women write more personally than men, even if they have had successful careers. They write more often than men of friends, spouses, and children.

The emphasis by women on the personal, especially on other people, rather than on their work life, their professional success, or their connectedness to current political or intellectual history clearly contradicts the established criterion about the content of autobiography.[2]

While Jelinek does not distinguish memoirs and autobiographies, she describes men's autobiographies as if they were memoirs, focussed on public roles and the writer's connection to historical events; the personal elements in women's autobiographies appear more consonant with expectations of that genre as a narrative of introspection. It might be that Holocaust memoirs do not follow the distinctions Jelinek finds because a memoir is not the same as an autobiography. However, some critics have seen the differences as minor: Marcus Billson and Sidonie Smith, writing of Lillian Hellman's memoirs, suggest that "the memorialist's vision of the outer world is as much a projection and refraction of the self as the autobiographer's. The manifest content of the memoir may be different, but the latent content is likewise self revelation."[3]

Although very little research has examined gender differences in the Holocaust, the question of the emotions of concentration camp inmates has elicited a few comments. The received wisdom has been that camp inmates' feelings became deadened through trauma and shock. Eugen Kogon and Alexander Donat have provided testimony in this vein; Donat writes (of Maidanek): "It was easier to get a piece of bread than a kind word."[4] Terrence Des Pres' compilation of survivor testimony echoes this judgment. However, Germaine Tillion, a French survivor of Ravensbrück, has denied that this response was as true for women as for men:

While some male prisoners aided their comrades for the highest motives, others did so as they became hardened to the necessity of the task, and many became cruel to the point of sadism, largely because of repressed sexual desires. In the women's camps, only the most selfish in character became so hardened, while for many the incredible personal suffering only increased their concern for the needs of others.[5]

Whether this statement and others like it can be supported by the memoirs of male and female survivors of other camps is one of the questions to be answered in this chapter. Were the women of Ravensbrück a special case because, as primarily a concentration camp for opponents of the Nazis, conditions were better than at Auschwitz?

Comparisons of inmate relations in Holocaust narratives may be made on the basis of patterns of assistance and support. Encounters in memoirs between the narrator-protagonist and other inmates, whether privileged or not, are typically either brief, fleeting contacts with strangers or acquaintances, or they are ongoing relationships based on friendship and/or family relationship. Both can be important events in survival stories. It is important to remember that the memoirist may create the reality: a "friend" named once and then dropped from the narrative may be in an ongoing relationship with the narrator, but the omission of the person from the rest of the narrative communicates that this is a fleeting contact, quite different from friendship.

The study of peer relations in Holocaust prose seems complicated by the variety of prisoner categories and situations which influence what can occur between deportees. Benedict Kautsky expresses it this way: "Even when you're talking about the same period of time, prisoners in the same camp lived as if on different planets, depending on the work they had to do." [6]

To find analogous pairs of male and female authored memoirs which can yield meaningful comparisons, several limitations need to be observed. It cannot be ignored that the discovery of exactly comparable situations among different inmates, even in the same camp, is impossible. However, one can reduce the extraneous elements by comparing death camp inmates only with other death camp inmates, rather than with inmates in camps devoted to the punishment of political prisoners. Furthermore, within the same camp, it makes little sense to compare ordinary inmates working primarily at outdoor manual labor with privileged inmates working in camp offices and thus freed from the hardest work, exposure to the weather, and frequent beatings; some privileged inmates also had access to additional food and clothing. Individual differences among privileged jobs seem less important than the fact that the individual's own struggle for survival could for significant stretches of time recede from being paramount. Divided into the two main groups of privileged and nonprivileged, the narratives can be questioned as to whether peer relations could contribute to survival.

Furthermore, Jewish prisoners should be compared with other Jews. Even though the differences of treatment are not always apparent, and Jews could suffer much less in privileged positions than some non-Jews in unprivileged positions, anti-semitism was the *raison d'être* of the death camps. This fact was obvious to Jewish prisoners, who were treated with significantly more brutality, selected for the gas chambers more often, and experienced much hatred from other inmates.

Two groups of Holocaust narratives can be distinguished among the texts discussed in the preceding chapters, on the basis of status in a camp and attitude toward other inmates:

1) Privileged and humanitarian, represented by Fania Fénelon, Judith Dribben, and sometimes Susan Schaeffer and Gerda Klein. Schaeffer's character Anya is privileged within a labor camp, but not before or after escape, periods which take up much space in the novel; Klein's status as weaver in labor camps is highly privileged except for certain cruel *kapos* in two of the camps.

2) Non-privileged and humanitarian, represented by Charlotte Delbo, a French political prisoner in Birkenau. A third cat-

egory, egocentric prisoners, either privileged or unprivileged, can be constructed, but pure examples are difficult to find, and none of the texts described previously belong to this group. But since many authors of memoirs define camp inmates this way, their memoirs can be imagined, if not often found.

To make comparisons between Holocaust memoirs by men and women, a selection of roughly analogous pairs needs to be made. Since not every woman's memoir has a male analogue readily available, some substitutions have been made in the interest of comparability. Fania Fénelon, as a privileged Jewish inmate of Birkenau (she was classed as Jewish although technically a half-Jew) can be compared with another privileged male Jewish inmate of Birkenau, the protagonist of *The Miracles Versus Tyranny* by Izaak Goldberg.[7] Judith Dribben, as a privileged and disguised Jew will not be discussed here. Charlotte Delbo's powerful memoir has been omitted from this discussion because of its uniqueness. For purposes of comparison, the memoirs *Night* by Elie Wiesel and *Elli* by Livia Bitton Jackson will represent unprivileged humanitarian survivors. These choices will be discussed further below. The tendency toward the egocentric memoir, which seems more available to certain male writers than to women, will be discussed as illustrated by Tadeusz Borowski's autobiographical short stories, *This Way for the Gas, Ladies and Gentlemen*.

The discussion is followed by some speculation to account for differences.

The following questions underlie the analysis of peer relations in the texts:

1. Did the protagonist try to help others? What possibilities existed for helping?

2. Did others help her or him? Close friends or others?

3. Does the author show concern between people through feelings or in some other way?

4. What is the role of the survivor's work or position in survival and possibilities of helping?

5. Does the memoir give evidence of uncomfortable feelings about survival in the present? Does this seem to affect the portrayal of helping?

6. What is the role of brief encounters or observation from a distance? What is the role of enduring relationships and friendships?

Privileged and Humanitarian

Fénelon's memoir *Playing for Time*, which was published in 1976 in the original French version, is that of a highly privileged survivor: a member of the Birkenau women's orchestra. Except for one or two days in the quarantine hut at the beginning and about five and one half months in Bergen-Belsen at the end, the memoir describes the author's eleven months (January to November, 1944) as a member of the Birkenau orchestra. Peer relations in this memoir focus upon conversations among orchestra members working and living crowded together, largely isolated from the ordinary inmates. However, the hostility of many non-privileged inmates toward the orchestra women is both implicitly and explicitly stated in the narrative and appears to be a motive for the writing of the book. Fénelon refers to the accounts of some survivors of the camp, "who had cast a shocked glance in our direction and retained in all good faith, only a subjective vision reflecting their feeling of the moment: envy, jealousy, anger, bitterness, or black humour?"[8] The memoir can be seen as a rebuttal to those who feel that the orchestra women were egocentric collaborators, but internal evidence also points to the author's own troubled feelings about the circumstances of her incarceration and survival. Most, though not all, of the encounters between the orchestra members and ordinary inmates are painful for Fénelon. Emblematic is Fénelon's description of the wretched inmates marching daily to outdoor work to the tune of a band composed of several orchestra members: "A look of hatred or scorn was like a knife wound; an insult was like being spat on."[9] Fénelon did not have to face these women daily, but several of her friends did; the orchestra functioned to make the system of terror operate more smoothly. At the conclusion of the ordeal, when the orchestra girls become unprivileged inmates in Bergen-Belsen, Fénelon reports singing Christmas carols in their block and receiving applause for the first time from the others. "It was the best present we could have had."[10]

Against the backdrop of the many women she was helpless

to save or assist, Fénelon focusses on the forty-seven women of the orchestra whom she was able to help. She portrays herself as the redeemer of the orchestra because of her musical talents, which she describes as superior to everyone except the *kapo*, Alma Rosé. By devoting her considerable knowledge to orchestrating pieces for them, she increases their repertoire and thus their ability to satisfy the SS' taste for music as a means of relaxation. She acknowledges that it is *Lagerführerin* Maria Mandel's love for an aria from Madame Butterfly which she can sing that allows her to be auditioned and saved in the first place. She also acknowledges one of the other French women who recognized her from having heard her sing at a French camp. But she emphasizes the value of her contribution to the orchestra as reflected in the initial joy of the members and the subsequent increase of her power and popularity within this group.

Fénelon portrays the help she gives the orchestra members in a series of dramatic scenes which often emphasize conflict between herself as main protagonist and other inmates who disagree with her. This style tends to emphasize her help as a series of measures to preserve the disintegrating morality of her peers. Although not egocentric, Fénelon's style is quite egotistical in the attention she gives herself. Apparently to prove that her survival was not just self-serving, she describes a variety of scenes in which her moral leadership is at first questioned but finally vindicated. Halfway through the memoir she assists Marta, the cello player, who is still recovering from typhus. This long-absent musician could play in that day's concert if her clothes were clean. As Fénelon begins to wash them in an automatic gesture of assistance, a chorus of French, German, and Polish voices condemns her act. They defend their practice of expecting everyone to manage on their own and resent Fénelon's arrogation of moral authority, which she feels is an act of kindness. "Who do you think you are? A Führer? We don't take lessons from anyone, and particularly not from you."[11] Fénelon's notion of the need for mutual assistance to make later life tolerable appears to fall on indifferent or hostile ears. The fact that disapproval of helping Marta crosses so many national boundaries suggests that it is not a matter of national rivalry or even personal selfishness, as Fénelon claims, but more likely the penetration of the

Nazi *Herrenmoral* among the inmates. The dominance of the strong over the weak apparently was practiced widely at Auschwitz as a determinant of prisoner relations.[12]

The same pattern recurs on an individual level in Fénelon's relationship to Clara, which begins as a vow of eternal friendship and mutual lifesaving (Clara prevents Fénelon from joining others in the "Red Cross" truck, unwittingly keeping her from the gas chambers; Fénelon gets Clara into the orchestra). As Clara becomes a *kapo's* whore to increase her food supply and finally a brutal *kapo* herself, Fénelon tries intermittently to remind her of former standards of behavior. The only effect is to uphold Fénelon as the consistent but ineffective defender of resistance against odds and to show that a corrupt environment has a power to transform some individuals in its own image, even among the privileged. In a reflective moment, Fénelon admits the underlying resemblance between herself and Clara; all of them were "suffering a sort of leprosy" in which "bits of oneself rotted and fell off without one's even knowing they'd gone."[13] But the narrator limits describing her own moral degeneration to the disgust she feels about singing and playing for the SS.

Despite her accusations of egocentrism among the women, the memoir also contains evidence for a more communal pattern of relations. Clara's prostitution is one self-centered response that disturbs Fénelon. More widely disliked are the Polish "Aryans" who abuse their status in the Nazi system at the expense of the others and throw away their surplus food while the rest go hungry (only the Polish "Aryans" and a few others could receive food packages from relatives). Loyalties which support the impression of community are strongest among compatriots or religious groups, although conflict within these groups often seems as apparent as the loyalties. Fénelon highlights several attachments among the musicians which transcend national and religious boundaries, such as her own friendship with Ewa, a Polish aristocrat who, like Fénelon, was active in the Resistance. She signals some spontaneous gestures of support at a moment of great need, such as Hilde and Helga, a Jewish and "Aryan" German, respectively, comforting Florette, a French Jew, when she returns after a particularly upsetting session of evening march music for brutalized inmates. The romance between

Marta, an aloof German Jew, and Little Irene, a French Communist, is accorded the major portion of a chapter. It allows Fénelon to show the triumph of love over squalor and cruelty, as well as her own function as trusted advisor, assuring them that "to the pure, all is pure."[14]

The help of friends continues in the Bergen-Belsen section even though there was no orchestra at this camp, with the result that Fénelon and the other musicians lose their privileged status. Some of the inmates have to perform manual labor; when Fénelon and Little Irene volunteer, Florette and Marta insist on replacing them because they are stronger. Fénelon receives extra food from her physician friend Marie and an opportunity to wash from Florette, now a *kapo*. Friendship retains its power as a conduit of survival help in deteriorating conditions.

While Fénelon's orchestrations and singing are at best an indirect form of solidarity with others, she describes one occasion when she is able to use her power to save a life. When she saves Florette from the wrath of their *kapo*, Sonia, by threatening suffocation if Sonia takes the thief of a few potatoes to the SS *Lagerführerin*, the reader can assume that the other musicians support Fénelon.[15] Without this support, the other players might have told the SS that she had murdered or was planning to kill their *kapo* during the night. Fénelon would not risk this if it were not extremely unlikely, since the orchestra members see their security linked to hers.

The orchestra's response to Fénelon's illness provides more evidence that the whole group is able to transcend sectarianism and contempt for the weak when the advantages are clear. The incident is described in *Sursis pour l'orchestre* but unfortunately withheld from *Playing for Time*.[16] While the incompetent Sonia is *kapo*, Fénelon becomes afflicted with painful vaginal abscesses. She must pretend to work in order to prevent Sonia or Mandel from sending her to the camp infirmary, the gateway to death. Fénelon directs her gratitude not only to her close friends, but also to all the others who keep silent, thus risking punishment. Even Founia, one of the "bestial" anti-semitic Poles, is so fearful of losing Fénelon and thus the orchestra that she is now making the bed of her ex-enemy. Although self-interest probably outweighs friendship in the motives of many of the musicians, the narrator acknowledges their generosity. The incident suggests a change of heart from the earlier incident with Marta, when the others failed to see the connection between help and self-interest. It also raises the possibility that self–interest and mutual assistance may be closely linked in many cases where this link is not stated.

Despite the conflict and argument which characterize many conversations recorded in the memoir, conflict does not usually contradict the impression of an underlying connection among many of the musicians. In part this is the result of humor, which punctuates arguments with great frequency, loosens apparently intransigent oppositions, and has a significant impact on morale.

Holocaust memoirs frequently end very shortly after liberation, after the survivor has ascertained family losses and, usually, decided on a new direction of some sort. Fénelon includes a final epilogue, "What Became of Us," which briefly describes the postwar fates of the women she knew. The inclusion of these two pages provides a sense of completion to the memoir and additional credence to Fénelon's concern with solidarity.

An approximate analogue to *Playing for Time* is *The Miracles Versus Tyranny* (1978), the memoir of Izaak Goldberg, M.D., a Jewish Polish physician who survived three Polish camps: Wolkowysk in Eastern Poland, Auschwitz-Birkenau, and Günthergrube, a Silesian camp belonging to Auschwitz III (Buna). (Goldberg adopts the name Dr. Harsaw in his story, presumably to protect his identity.)[17] Medical work was among the most favored occupations for those working in the Nazi camps. While conditions for physicians were not identical to those for the orchestra members, they, like musicians, owed their privileged survival to their occupations when they were allowed to work as caretakers in the barracks or doctors in the hospital. Although carrying out this work was morally less ambiguous than playing music for the SS, it was full of its own contradictions: hospitals were frequently antechambers to death, devoid of medicines or supplies, targets of frequent selections for the gas chambers, and subject to every whim of the SS. Medical personnel had to use considerable ingenuity and risk in order to save lives, even temporarily.

Harsaw refrains from moral judgments against his fellow prisoners, and they apparently have nothing but a high regard for him. This is certainly credible during his year at Birkenau, where he exerts great effort to treat sick inmates and saves many people at considerable risk. At Günthergrube, to which he is sent as punishment for hiding Jewish patients from selections at Birkenau, he is saved from hard outdoor labor by a German construction supervisor. The man's connections to high Nazi officials allow Harsaw to become the man's private physician without recrimination from the camp administration. Because of this connection, other inmates hold him in high esteem. He expresses no moral qualms about being the personal physician of the German "Master" architect of Günthergrube, whose peptic ulcer he cures. Neither does he reveal any animosity from unprivileged inmates. Harsaw's only reference to the ethics of the situation is that he refuses to drink vodka with the Master to celebrate their acquaintance.

Harsaw's survival story describes the struggle to work as a Jewish physician in Birkenau as a combination of initiative, help, and divine miracles. At the time of his arrival in Birkenau, thirty-five doctors from his and a preceding transport are allowed to enter the camp. Many others, still sick from typhus contracted in the preceding camp of Wolkowysk, are gassed immediately. On Harsaw's ninth day in the camp, five doctors are selected to be *Pflegers* (caretakers) of various barracks, among them Dr. Harsaw. A *Pfleger's* duties were primarily housekeeping chores in a barracks. All of the remaining thirty are abandoned to the ordinary fate and death within a few weeks.[18] Of these Harsaw mentions only one, Dr. Epstein, who survives by getting a *Pfleger* job on his own initiative. Those who have officially been assigned the job of *Pfleger* must struggle to keep these jobs and their lives.

Harsaw's one year in Birkenau involves frequent moves from one barracks to another. This unsettled aspect of his camp existence derives both from the extermination policy of the camp administration and from Harsaw's initiative to function as a doctor. Whatever the cause, transfers to safer or better positions involve the assistance of comrades but shorten the time that prisoners spend working and living together. Because their first job as caretaker of various barracks terminates unexpectedly by an administrative order, Harsaw and two other Jewish doctors land in a barrack where they face plentiful mistreatments. As one of the *Pflegers* has told Harsaw immediately after arrival, many of them are targets of beatings from Block Elders and other officials. Harsaw is able to escape this torment because his friend Katzengold from his last barrack helps him to get a job registering new arrivals in his own bookkeeping commando (work group). Mr. Aleks, a veteran prisoner and dental technician, helps Harsaw later to move from a *Pfleger* position in Barrack 16 to a similar job in Barrack 8, which is to become a "real hospital." Harsaw tells his fellow Wolkowysk doctor Kaplan about the openings in Block 8, and Kaplan is also accepted.

Harsaw mentions these friends (Katzengold and Aleks) in passing as he tells about his own struggle to survive and does not mention them again. Another friend from his home town, Dr. Epstein, is described much at first, then disappears from the narrative. Harsaw records conversations in which he encourages Epstein to maintain his spirit. Then he reports that Epstein is not accepted back into a *Pfleger* job after losing the first one, because he is "short and weak." Later he organizes food for Epstein, saying that although his own food was inadequate, he "had to save him." This occurs on page 295. Harsaw mentions Epstein next sixty-one pages later in a list of doctors working in the new hospital complex. Harsaw does not mention Epstein further, although the memoir goes on another 235 pages![19]

This disappearance of friends and acquaintances from the narrative without a trace is a recurrent characteristic of *The Miracles Versus Tyranny*. Important concrete help is exchanged with various men, and then they drop out of sight. The men who help Harsaw do not in general figure again in the narrative as enduring friends. Names bob out of the ocean of prisoners and events only to disappear forever. The impression of the importance of friends is mixed: the practical help given is important, but not the friendships. The only exceptions prove the rule: for example, Dr. Kaplan, from whom Harsaw obtains a favor later as part of a scheme to save an inmate's life, is otherwise absent from the text. Most of the people whose eventual survival is clearly asserted are patients whom Harsaw saves. These include Zapolanski, a carpenter from Wolkowysk, whose number an inmate doctor removes from the death list at Harsaw's request after Harsaw operates on the man's leg; Mr. B.I., whom Harsaw helps to avoid sterilization by telling him to keep the electrode on his thigh rather than his testicles; Itzkowitz, a relative of Harsaw, who is removed from the holding block for the gas chamber (he has a small leg lesion) because a *Schreibstube* friend of Harsaw agrees to put his "head in the lion's mouth," in hopes for Harsaw's friendship when the expected final liquidation occurs.[20] (But Harsaw does not mention him again!)

The fragmentary pattern of relationships is echoed in the oscillation of the narrative between Harsaw's personal story and chronicle of World War II battles. Harsaw does not account for this. He seems to enjoy leaving the enclosure of the camp at intervals to follow the course of the war, at times suggesting connections, such as increased or decreased SS brutality, depending upon the fortunes of the German army.

Although Harsaw is able to use his privileged position to the advantage of many prisoners, his relations with them remain primarily pragmatic and detached. He does not describe much involvement with his patients. His interactions with other physicians demonstrate a concern that seems ineffective against an overwhelming despair. Medicines and surgery, when he can exploit them, are useful, but encouragement seems largely powerless. Having gotten his first job in Barrack 17, he has conversations with several other men who have sunk into pre-suicidal despair. Many of them commit suicide by going to the medical clinic, where the infamous Polish doctor Zentkeller sends them to Block 7 to wait for the gas chamber trucks. Harsaw's words are of no use against this despair. After encountering the ex-chief of the Judenrat of Wolkowysk, he reminds him of the many trials they have endured in one month at Birkenau, telling him that the Germans are retreating from Russia and that the war will probably be over soon. But "the proud Fucks" leaves him in tears.[21] He meets a former neighbor from Wolkowysk, Nahum Olszevski, who has survived three months in the camp through the help of a friend who was a foreman. "But now, I am sick and very weak. All my body is swollen. I am not going to last much longer. I'll go tomorrow to the clinic. Dr. Zenkteller [*sic*] will send me to Block Seven and my Suffering [*sic*] will be finished."[22] Harsaw reveals his own similar inability to believe in encouragement when he has lost his preferred status. While he is awaiting transfer from Birkenau to Günthergrube, other veteran inmates give him extra food, tell prisoner officials not to bother him, tell him to hide from selections, and encourage him with the information that he will be helping to construct a new camp for the first six months, by which time the war might be over. However, depression and the logic of ultimate extermination are stronger than friendly advice. Only the feel of his medical diploma in his pocket gives Harsaw a feeling of some safety, since it has represented security until now. It is more equivocal than the advice, however; the advice could be used, whereas for the time being the diploma will remain powerless against the authorities' aim to punish Harsaw by depriving him of official appointment to any physician position.

In Günthergrube friendship becomes somewhat more important to Harsaw. Weinberg, a Pole with whom Harsaw shares a barrack and an outdoor labor detail, has an impressive range of knowledge to which he lays claim, probably all the more impressive to Harsaw, a physician denied the possibility to exercise his skill. Their dialogue consists almost entirely of conversations about escape from the camp, or Weinberg's descriptions of Janowska, a much worse camp, intended to convince Harsaw that they must escape. In the end, however, the two escape separately from the evacuation out of Günthergrube, but meet again after the liberation. Their conversations seem to have a concealed emotional function as distraction from camp reality. After liberation, Weinberg persuades Harsaw to come with him to Katowice instead of going back to Wolkowysk, where Harsaw would find only absences of parents, siblings, and relatives. In this very concealed manner, Harsaw seems to suggest a family-like bonding with his friend, but it is all quite unemotional.

Harsaw also becomes the protector of a prisoner in Günthergrube. He is able to use his "high esteem" among the prisoner elite to provide a man from his home town with an easy job as electrician and later as a *kapo* of a mine group. But no friendship is described; in fact Szerezewski does not offer Harsaw any of his improved food supply and pretends not to see him in the camp. Harsaw protests a bit too much that he doesn't mind, finds the man amusing and an education in "human deportment." Nevertheless, when Harsaw decides to escape the evacuation march, it is this man who escapes with him.

Some of the most important of Harsaw's prisoner relations remain abstract, because men he does not know well haunt his conscience. He describes the execution of five innocent prisoners by the camp elder because of an alleged *desire* to escape. Inexplicably, Harsaw escapes punishment for the identical charge—he is detained inside the camp after an informer fabricates a story about his fictional escape plans. Harsaw never identifies his feelings as guilt. He is plainly obsessed with the issue, however, as he calls the five victims saints, hypothesizes about why he was never punished, and rails against the light postwar sentences given to the camp elder Alois Frey and other Nazis.

Fénelon and Harsaw both describe prisoner assistance in Birkenau. Both are able to use their positions to help other inmates, but Harsaw has the advantage because of the nature of his medical work. Both seem to have enduring friendships, but Fénelon describes hers more and ascribes much more emotional importance to them. She describes them as longer lasting and more connected to the ability to maintain hope during imprisonment. Harsaw's bonds with men he saves at risk to himself seem more important to him in his postwar life than in the camps.

Fénelon and Harsaw are both privileged prisoners at Birkenau, and both experience transfer to another camp where they are not privileged. They both write about heroic assistance which emphasizes their own actions so that they present themselves as morally equal to the gift of survival. But the differences in their jobs at Birkenau make conclusions about possible male-female differences in group survival patterns quite tentative. Harsaw's medical work affords more opportunities to help ordinary inmates, even though drugs are lacking, whereas Fénelon's possibilities to help are apparently limited to the considerably privileged orchestra members. In addition, the great contrast between the relative stability of the orchestra block and the constant fluctuation of prisoner doctors from block to block in Harsaw's experience likely have an effect upon the character of peer relations, such as the difference in the development of friendship.

Since there are memoirs by female physician survivors of Birkenau, it is not difficult to find out if a memoir by such a survivor supports the contrast between Harsaw and Fénelon. Gisella Perl's *I Was a Doctor in Auschwitz* (1948) offers a glimpse into the women's camp in Birkenau.[23] Perl, a Hungarian doctor deported in April or May, 1944, mentions three different work stations in Birkenau but emphasizes the hospital where she worked several months.

Perl's description of obtaining her job as physician differs from both Harsaw and Fénelon. Harsaw struggles to get and keep his positions as *Pfleger* and physician; Fénelon highlights proving herself in a formal audition and orchestrating without much prior experience. Perl takes her medical status for granted, never actually mentioning the moment when the authorities appoint her to an official position. An SS official's order to her as a doctor to calm "these animals" (the entering women inmates) is not followed by any indication that her official capacity begins here. Her initiation and functioning seem to develop almost organically out of situations and her feelings for the other women. After her experience of performing an abortion on (bisexual) SS woman Irma Grese and unexpectedly surviving this (touching a guard was punishable by death but so was refusing an order!), she resolves to devote her life in camp to helping the other women. By portraying her official appointment as something taken for granted, she minimizes her heroic dimensions while fulfilling a selfless, maternal role in her professional relation to the other inmates.

Perl clearly has medical skills equivalent to Harsaw which help her to save numerous lives in Birkenau. The lack of drugs and instruments increases the impression of skill and commitment to preserving life against odds when she operates on infected breasts with only a knife and delivers many women in all stages of pregnancy with only her bare hands, thus saving them from death. When comparing Harsaw and Perl, however, the quite different role of conversation and feelings is striking. Perl makes many claims for the power of encouragement and tender words in helping, even healing, sick women. Harsaw makes the opposite claim: words have no power against prisoners who say they have lost hope. Although he once mentions encouraging his patients, he accords vastly more significance to other strategies like substituting numbers on the lists, organizing medicines, and hiding sick prisoners from the SS. Aside from keeping sick people from entering the hospital, Perl does not mention these tactics and as a later arrival to the camp probably lacks the contacts with the "Canada" workers to organize medicines. Instead, she emphasizes placebos and the power of her words as an authority figure. For example, she creates a psychological miracle by declaring that margarine can cure skin diseases and, when it actually works, causes the price of margarine in the camp black market to soar above everything else. Faced constantly with great misery and no real drugs, she relies again and again on words, which apparently have some effect. She describes how the SS use weak women prisoners to extract blood plasma for the German army (inconsistently ignoring their law against racial pollution), and how the inmate doctors are ordered to "put these women back on their feet." Amazingly, with nothing but "words, encouragement, tenderness," the drained women come back to life.[24]

Dr. Perl also describes at great length her friendships with other doctors in the hospital block. Living and working together with eight other women, Perl describes their community in ideal terms: she says they share a similar cultural and social background, interests and ideals. They are able to help each other to endure hunger and Dr. Mengele's beatings by singing songs and talking about literature. (Here Perl's account differs from many others which describe conversations primarily about food: recipes and imaginary meals.) They form a family in which they pool the food they earn from "private" patients, sometimes going without this bonus ration in order to pay for someone's needed shoes, etc. Within this group, Perl describes her closer sustaining friendships with Olga Schwartz, a pediatrician friend from two years previous. She also describes her supportive relationship with Olga Singer, her nurse and assistant in Dege Werke, a labor camp in Hamburg.

Because of the primacy of feelings in the memoir, Perl seems less heroic and egocentric than Harsaw. The mutuality of feelings between physician and patients—many of whom become her friends—gives the message that Perl is able to gratify a need to nurture and be nurtured by her patients. Like Fénelon and Harsaw, however, saving lives gives Perl a moral justification for survival even though both her husband and son were killed.

Although Perl stresses her humanitarian role with others, like Fénelon, she describes a background of battling women in the camp, from which she wishes to disassociate herself.

There was only one law in Auschwitz—the law of the jungle—the law of self-preservation. Women who in their former lives were decent, self-respecting human beings now stole, lied, spied, beat the others and—if necessary—killed them, in order to save their miserable lives.[25]

A gulf separates these frantic struggling women and Perl's idyllic hospital enclave, an even greater gulf, it seems, than that between Fénelon's often arguing orchestra members and the "others" of Birkenau. Harsaw is silent about the egotism of the inmates in the men's camp; it is simply not an issue for him.

The power of mutual help in the camps is discounted by Lawrence Langer in *Versions of Survival*.[26] He cites, among others, Ella Lingens-Reiner, a German political prisoner and a physician at Birkenau, who finds herself in a seemingly insoluble moral dilemma when trying to save someone's life. She reports that since a fixed quota of inmates was scheduled to be gassed, the removal of one inmate's number meant the substitution of someone else's number.[27] It is true that this practice lessens the efficacy of acts of lifesaving. Many survivors, including all those discussed above, leave the information out of their narratives, implying that it does not exist or that they are unaware of it. (Do they know?) But the intrinsic moral value of saving someone's life against odds remains, despite the unchanging numbers of the gas chamber quotas. The emotional climate of the camp environment contained pockets of human caring, in part because some inmates with connections to the camp elite could initiate efforts to have names removed from the lists. Lingens-Reiner, despite her own frustration at the unprecedented situation, asserts that "sometimes one must do things for their own sake without regard for their actual results."[28]

Less Privileged Inmates

Although Charlotte Delbo's memoir has rich descriptions of peer relations for unprivileged inmates, it is very difficult to find an appropriate analogue by a man for comparison. An analogue to Delbo would have to be a male non-Jewish political prisoner, preferably French, condemned to ordinary outside labor at Birkenau for at least several months. Delbo's status places her chances above those of the Jews, and although the moment-by-moment suffering seems often the same, other factors argue against comparability. Jews were beaten more, selected more often for the gas chambers, and were often faced with linguistic isolation when housed with Jews of different nationalities. It seems that Delbo's situation was worse than many other political prisoners, whose political contacts enabled them to find protected jobs sooner.[29]

Less privileged inmates of Auschwitz and other camps owe their survival to their work only in so far as it keeps them from being killed immediately. "Unprivileged" is a relative category; such prisoners usually become factory workers or find indoor work eventually because long periods of outdoor labor by low-status inmates are not consistent with survival in the Nazi death camps. Even a few weeks of outdoor work in a bad labor group is a long time to endure exhausting work coupled with starvation, exposure to weather, and beatings. If these prisoners find indoor work, they win greater stability in conditions and protection from the weather but still have to stand in morning and evening roll calls, may be subject to the whims of bad *kapos*, must endure selections, and usually receive the same wretched food as the outdoor laborers. These torments do not afflict privileged prisoners or affect them far less.

The similarities of *Night* by Elie Wiesel and *Elli* by Livia Bitton Jackson make a strong claim to their suitability for comparison of less privileged inmates.[30] As memoirs by Hungarian survivors, they are both accounts of a relatively late date of deportation, late spring, 1944. Both survivors, however, experience the murderous conditions of the evacuations from Auschwitz before the Russian advance. Both Jackson and Wiesel enter Auschwitz as teenagers accompanying their same-sex parents, and both are separated from and lose other family members, including their opposite-sex parents. Both survivor memoirists have orthodox Jewish cultural backgrounds which affect their experience and recording of the event. Added to this, both pairs of survivors are transferred from Birkenau fairly quickly to labor camps. On the other hand, an important difference between the two pairs is that Elli and her mother move around more, staying in five camps—Birkenau C-Lager, Plaszow, Birkenau B-Lager, Augsburg, and Mühldorf—as opposed to Wiesel and his father's three camps: Birkenau, Auschwitz I, and Buna. Since the focus of this discussion is on the parent-child relationships, and both pairs stay together throughout the moves, the difference is not crucial.

Hermann Langbein (*Menschen in Auschwitz*) says that younger people in Auschwitz were physically more resilient and accepted more quickly than older inmates the Nazi *Herrenmoral*, which prescribed contempt and worse treatment for all weaker inmates by the stronger ones.[31] However, he does not describe boys with their fathers in the camps, or daughters with their mothers. The memoirs of Elie Wiesel and Livia Bitton Jackson do not entirely agree with Langbein's claim about juvenile accommodation to Nazi attitudes. While Wiesel's portrait of his father confirms the physical vulnerability of the elderly, and he mentions sons who abandon their fathers when conditions worsen, his own relationship to his father is basically loyal. Jackson's view of Auschwitz, while more like Wiesel than Langbein, takes its own route, as we shall see.

As Wiesel enters Birkenau with his fifty-year-old father, after his mother and three sisters disappear forever on the other side of the Auschwitz ramp, young Elie Wiesel vows never to be separated from his father. This thought accompanies the then almost fifteen-year-old boy throughout his account of Auschwitz work, selections, and transports. In a sense, the memoir documents the boy's victory over strong pressures toward separation in the camps, as his father dies shortly before liberation with his son still close to him. In describing other sons who

abandon their weakened fathers in the end or fight with them
to death over a piece of bread, Wiesel places himself in the
different category of those who manage to survive with the
essence of their former morality intact. But the enduring to-
getherness of Wiesel and his father is qualified by emotional
distance and a minimum of mutual nurturance.

Wiesel indicates that his father's emotional distance is a continuation of his former life and not only a product of camp
hardships. After eight days in Auschwitz, a man named Stein,
a Belgian relative of Wiesel, finds the two of them and asks for
information about his family. Wiesel's father does not recognize
this husband of his wife's niece, and the author relates this non-
recognition to his father's preoccupation with the Jewish affairs
of their town and his lack of emotional display to his family.
Young Wiesel fills the vacuum by lying to Stein with news from
his family to lift his morale, thus prolonging the man's life until
he gets real news. Wiesel's father says nothing in the text, unable
to duplicate the family reunions of other male inmates.

Wiesel develops the theme of isolation between father and
son in the telling of other incidents. Both suffer beatings in camp
which elicit an awareness of powerlessness and guilt in the author. When a Gypsy strikes his father to the ground right after
their arrival, Wiesel reports his remorse at having failed to defend his father, as he would have normally, and the father,
guessing his son's feelings, says that it does not hurt. When the
father is beaten later more severely by another *kapo*, the son's
response is to protect himself and to feel angry at his father for
not avoiding the blows. "That is what concentration camp life
had made of me."[32] After Elie endures twenty-five lashes at the
hands of another *kapo*, he thinks of his father probably suffering
more than he himself. In neither case does Wiesel indicate assistance between son or father; it is simply absent.

The absence of conversation between Wiesel and his father is
striking in the memoir. It is as if they lack the language to break
a silence which entraps them. The memoir suggests a reason for
this is the loss of the faith which they once shared, which seems
to shatter the older man's will to live. On Rosh Hashanah, Jewish
New Year's Day, he seems most beaten; Wiesel says, "We had

never understood one another so clearly" although their communion at the time remains silent.[33]

Wiesel describes his hospital surgery on a foot that has swollen from working in the winter cold at Buna. Although the operation is serious, he does not mention any visit from his father. Are visits not allowed as in Jackson's *Elli*? Wiesel does not say. He only refers to his own ability to help his father by sending him some of his extra bread ration. The stay in the hospital represents a respite from the camp—better food, no work or roll calls. Yet the hospital's frequent selections are a danger of which Elie learns from his dying bedmate.

Some understated feeling is expressed when the father believes he has been selected to die, moments before his son must march off on a work brigade. In what they believe to be their last conversation, Wiesel says he suppresses a sob and, since there will be a second selection process, tries to convince his father to keep his knife and spoon, not to give them to him. At work Elie feels "sick at heart" and "in a trance." Wiesel calls the subsequent reunion with his reprieved father a miracle but otherwise remains on the level of facts: "I gave him back his knife and spoon."[34]

Even the exclusively practical help which some accounts have attributed to male camp inmates is extremely limited between father and son in *Night*. In Buna the elder Wiesel forbids his son to fast on Yom Kippur but otherwise plays no visible role in feeding or clothing his son. Most of the helping between them occurs during the evacuation march. The father and son keep each other awake when exhaustion and snow make sleep very dangerous. When a nameless prisoner tries to strangle Elie on an open wagon, the father calls a friend who still has strength to beat off the attacker. Wiesel helps his father primarily when he can somewhat lessen the older man's torment while dying by bringing him food and water (at the end of the march, the sick get no rations). One concludes from this memoir that even practical help between family members is often negligible in the camps, and only rarely sustains life.

Wiesel reveals his ambivalence about staying with his father in the final days of the march. At first his commitment to staying together almost gets him killed when he tries to stay with his father in a selection; while the SS try to stop him, the resulting chaos allows both of them and others to escape. As his father deteriorates toward death, Wiesel reveals a gap between thoughts and actions. Separated from his father at Buchenwald, the desire not to find him again crosses his mind—to be able to fight for his own survival. As Elie gives him the remainder of his soup, he feels "a heavy heart." The fact that he does remain loyal to his father, despite a *kapo's* reproach that he should be eating his father's ration, not giving him his own, represents a victory over the environment of amorality. Wiesel's honesty about his ambivalence seems to suggest both survival guilt and the assertion, in the camp, of an egocentric will to survive.

What in Wiesel's *Night* is a recurrent prayer of the teenager not to be separated from his father, is in Jackson's *Elli* a desperate cry motivated by an inner necessity. The closer emotional tie of the mother-daughter bond is apparent in the lengths to which they go to stay together, especially the efforts of the daughter. Although the mother's age is not stated, she seems younger than Wiesel's father, a real advantage. The accident which she suffers in Birkenau, while not equal to the elder Wiesel's suffering on the evacuation, implies a longer dependence of parent on child. The mother-child bond is tighter and more resistant to the onslaughts of the camp than the father-son bond in Wiesel.

As in *Night* the narrative is focussed on the child narrator's need to stay with the parent. What is different is that the force of the need becomes more credible because of the obstacles that it transcends. In addition, the female parent is able to continue her maternal role longer in camp life and in extreme conditions. There is more conflict between mother and daughter because sacrifices by the parent are too upsetting to the child, or vice versa. Other adults in the camps who offer Elli protection confirm the greater readiness of women to take care of another prisoner, continuing their roles as nurturers. But Jackson leaves out descriptions of friendships for the most part, as she omits much reference to the aggressions of women and girls fighting each other over food. The mother-child drama, except for the inclusion of her brother at brief intervals, overshadows everything else in Auschwitz.

Elli reveals a specific motive for so intensely wanting to protect her mother: she insists that if her mother dies, she will not be able to endure it; she herself will die. Since her mother survives, no direct proof exists, but Jackson provides indirect evidence. When their outdoor work unit at Camp Plaszow is caught at "sabotage" (seeking shelter during a rainstorm), the punishment of decimation (the shooting of every tenth inmate) awaits them at dawn. Elli's terror is greater when envisioning her mother's body falling into a pool of blood than when she imagines her own bullet ridden body. She weeps hysterically and insists that they stay awake all night, to be together every moment left to them. (The decimation is called off mysteriously.)

Elli's reactions to her mother's injury and illness provide evidence that great personal courage can arise from the belief that someone else's survival is necessary to one's own. After being injured and paralyzed by a fallen bed plank in Birkenau Lager B, their third camp, Mrs. Friedmann spends over a month in the camp infirmary. Her daughter illegally haunts the Revier (hospital) and finds a loose knothole through which she can talk with her mother. (Visiting the sick is forbidden.) Against prediction, Mrs. Friedmann gets better, surely in part connected to this support. Caught loitering near this building, Elli has to kneel on gravel without food or water for twenty-four hours. Although she is under threat of being gassed if caught again, she saves her mother from an imminent selection in the Revier. Elli and her "adoptive" family Mrs. Grünwald, her daughter Ilse, and Yituka carry her at great risk from the infirmary to the barrack. Inmates are forbidden to walk even to the latrine without SS escort.

Although Elli's brother Bubi has an elite position as interpreter in Auschwitz and can bring them food, the threat of selections makes exit from Auschwitz the only safe course for Mrs. Friedmann. An imminent transport of prisoners to work in German factories provides the answer. Supported by her daughter, then grabbed by the official, the paralyzed mother passes selection, while the daughter, afflicted with a festering leg sore (she has never mentioned it before), does not pass. All that she can think of is the danger to her mother, too weak to do anything by herself. Faced with this intolerable separation (not by the possibility of being gassed), Elli ignores the promise of another woman's care and sneaks into her mother's transport when the official isn't looking. Having found her mother in the shower, she sees an SS woman grab her mother's arm and twist it, because Laura Friedmann's efforts to dress herself with paralyzed hands are too slow. Elli, oblivious to all but the danger to her mother, jumps at the SS woman and, shouting to leave her alone, shoves her against the wall. By all odds, the result should be Elli's death. By some chance of fate, the SS woman merely kicks and punches her severely all over her body. When Elli gets on the train bound for Augsburg with her mother, she acknowledges that "a sense of triumph overwhelms the pain."[35] It is a movement toward life because the factory in Augsburg offers much better conditions and a chance for the mother to recover most of her functions.

Jackson's memoir includes a few illustrations of her mother's care of her in the camps in scenes which precede or follow her period of illness. When her mother makes any sacrifice to play a protective role, the daughter asserts that she can hardly bear it. In Plaszow when Elli and her mother have to work in the stone brigade, Mrs. Friedmann passes only small stones to her, but skips her when they have to pass larger rocks. The narrator calls it dreadful to see her mother leaning forward, holding a heavy rock while the girl beyond Elli has to lean down to reach the rock. The mother ignores her daughter's insistence that she also pass the large rocks, unknowingly making the work an emotional trauma for her daughter.

An event with similar implications is a unique fight over food between mother and daughter in Augsburg. On the fifth day of Passover, Elli is one of eight inmates punished because they hid from having to work outside coatless in freezing weather. Having taken liquids but no bread for several days to observe the festival, Elli must stand silently with others until late evening without food. As her mother is in poorer physical condition than she, Elli refuses to eat more than half of the bowl of soup her mother has saved from her supper. Her mother insists that Elli must eat it all. When Elli resists, her mother turns the bowl over onto the bed, spilling the contents. Driven to desperation by this mutual concern for each other in their need, they both lose a precious meal and spend the night weeping in each other's arms. This portrayed unwillingness to receive protection at someone else's expense is uncommon in any memoir. But it represents the possibility of the conservation of female symbiotic nurturing patterns despite an environment often described as a war of egos. It sometimes seems as if some women, such as Elli and her mother, cling more strongly to each other in the environment of such a battleground. Certainly, the narrator of *Elli* makes a strong case that for many women such islands of caring are essential for their survival.

The evacuation of the Mühldorf inmates in *Elli* confirms the impressions gained in the other parts of the memoir. During the six-day boxcar ride, which is mostly devoid of food or water, memorable moments include a false liberation which ends in machine gun fire, when Mrs. Friedmann searches for her son in the train before thinking of finding food; and her cradling of her son's wounded head in her lap, oblivious to SS machine gun fire as she finds refuge from the violence and hunger in a familiar role.

While both memoirs emphasize a teenager's task of staying together with a weaker parent in several camps, the persona of Jackson's narrator seems much younger than that of Wiesel. Wiesel's age is about two years older than Jackson's in the Holocaust, but Wiesel's narrator sounds like an adult looking back, while Jackson's narrator has the naive immediacy of a young girl and appears to unfold in the present. Jackson even uses the present tense more. Wiesel speaks of staying with his father as a responsibility as well as a need. Elli refers to staying with her mother as her chief survival strategy, because her need for her is greater than anything else. It is impossible to say that Elli's mother survived only because of her daughter, or that Wiesel's father would have survived had Wiesel done something else for him. The parents' ages and the circumstances are too different. The difference in the way they describe other people is also striking: Wiesel gives to his portrayal of his relationship to his father a background of other despondent old men and desperate sons. Jackson provides little about other mothers and daughters, mentioning other women only rarely. She does not find it necessary or perhaps morally acceptable to dwell on the predominant egocentrism of the camps except in a rare descriptive phrase such as the "uncaring madness of Auschwitz."

Egocentric Survivors

Is there such a thing as an egocentric main protagonist in a Holocaust memoir? Apparently the tendency against such a phenomenon is very strong. The moral imperative which powers many acts of bearing witness seems to preclude showing much egocentrism. Even accounts which strive for detached objectivity usually include some description of helping or friendship. Memoirs by many privileged survivors, like Fénelon and Goldberg, often feature the self in dramatic acts of assistance, making the most of every possible opportunity to exchange help.

One book which takes a different approach is the collection of autobiographical short stories by Tadeusz Borowski, *This Way for the Gas, Ladies and Gentlemen.*[36] Borowski's apparent aim of revealing the corrupting influence of the system on the inmates limits the prevalence of helping and friendship as a theme. The awareness of amorality is still present, and moments of helping and friendship exist, but they are often subordinate to a different aim.

The glimpses of egocentrism of the narrator and other inmates can be seen in their attitude toward the gas chamber victims and toward friendships with each other. They have the awareness that survival and friendship, the good life of well-off prisoners at Auschwitz, depend upon the train transports bringing European Jews to their deaths. These facts arouse little moral response in most of them, and if the narrator is more troubled about them than others, he too admits that he prefers to live than to be overly concerned by the fate of the others. While working with his friend Henri clearing the boxcars of victims and their belongings, the narrator is so overcome by terror, nausea, and fury at the victims that he must retreat to recover nearby. At this moment, he thinks of the camp as a haven of peace where "others may be dying, but one is somehow still alive, one has enough food, enough strength to work."[37]

Friendship in Borowski's stories is also an ironic concept. He uses the word but often attributes unaccustomed meanings to it. At the beginning of the story named above, the narrator and several others sit on their bunks, eating a meal: Borowski eats from his packages from home while the others eat food from the "cremo transports" (crematorium transports), the main supply of the French, Jews, and Russians. Borowski's French friend Henri says that, if the transports stopped, they would not let the Poles eat their food packages in peace. (Their hunger would be overwhelming.) Tadeusz replies that they would starve like the Greeks. Prior to this, he says they have been friends a long time, but he does not know Henri's last name. It is a provisional friendship, based upon an abundant food supply, which in turn is based upon a camp class system founded upon privilege for Poles and the stolen food of Jewish victims.

Another of Borowski's striking uses of the word "friend" is his explanation of the transfer of part of "Canada" to one of the hardest labor squads: When the powerful lose power and status, "their friends see to it that they fall to the very bottom."[38] What kind of friends are these? These and other examples imply that friendship is a word with quite ironic meanings in Auschwitz.

It is not that Borowski is completely friendless. He refers to various friends by name. He roams around the camp with two other Poles, one of whom, Staszek, has good contacts in the kitchens and supply rooms. These contacts give him food in return for past help, and he shares it with the other two. There are other instances of assistance, too. But Borowski's style de-mythologizes and flattens all of these moments, so that they appear to be barely significant moments in a time flux dominated by participation in evil as if it were ordinary life. The text conveys a double vision: the dulled sensibilities of the moment-by-moment everyday living in the camp; and the moral perspective of the creator of these scenes, often invisible but not always.

Conclusion in Light of Psychoanalytic Theory

The comparisons of Holocaust memoirs by men and women show that they do not write in the same way about their relationships with other inmates in the camps. It is not possible to make absolutely reliable inferences about actual events from memoirs, but the act of remembering the past is related to wider behavior, and both are partly affected by gender roles. The memoirs and related autobiographical narratives show that women feature the value of friendship and relationship in the camps much more than men. While both men and women write about important help given to and received from other people in the camps, they do not dramatize equally the way they write about this help. Many memoirists of both sexes emphasize the help they give more than the help they receive, thus emphasizing their moral fitness as survivors and dealing in this way with survival guilt. Men, however, most consistently feature strategic and pragmatic mutual assistance while apparently omitting reference to emotional support, or denying the effectiveness of such support. As a result, rather than denying the need for support, men's memoirs reveal more depression about the situation of the inmates than do women's memoirs. Conversation as a way to maintain hope and community in inhuman conditions is a decisive feature of women's memoirs; it is much less prevalent or powerful in men's memoirs as a bonding device. Men describe their relationships with each other as much less permanent than females do. Even though men and women are moved from one camp to another or from one barracks to another, women's relationships seem less fragmented. Finally, although in general women express more feelings in their memoirs, they express less anger at each other than men reveal. What has been described as a universal adoption by inmates of Nazi values of domination of the weak is apparently much less true for women than for men in memoirs.

Trying to account for these differences has many pitfalls since the theories which attempt to explain human behavior presuppose an ideal condition of "normal" conditions, which the Holocaust does not fulfill. However, ordinary life is less uniform than often supposed; "choiceless choices," a term which Lawrence Langer has applied to conditions in the camps, is also a feature of many less advantaged people, as Joan Ringelheim has pointed out.[39]

Why do men and women write Holocaust memoirs with marked differences in the ties between prisoners? They endure the same work, the same starvation, the same crowding, filth, and threat of death, but they write differently about their need for other inmates and their capacities to benefit from them. Some recent feminist reappropriations of psychoanalytic theory may shed some light on the differences in male and female versions of remembering camp experiences. Nancy Chodorow's *The Reproduction of Mothering* (1978) has received considerable attention as an explanation of the greater capacities for relationship and empathy in women, as well as the perpetuation of primary parenting by females.[40] This theory has applications to the writing of Holocaust memoirs by women and suggests that the relationship differences in these documents have a basis in the different psychic structures produced by the patriarchal family.

Chodorow reinterprets Freud's analysis of the Oedipus complex from the point of view of the mother to analyze the reproduction of social relations within the family. Following Adler's object relations theory, she explains that the infant initially does not distinguish between the "I" and the "not-I" for the first year of life and experiences itself as psychologically and physically fused with its mother. But as the male infant grows older, mothers and sons experience each other as sexual opposites, and by the time the boy enters the Oedipus complex, he is supposed to reject his primary attachment to his mother in order to overcome a conflict with his father by identifying with him. Mothers experience their daughters as more like them and more continuous with themselves. Girls do not have to give up their primary attachment to their mothers as much as boys do and tend to retain this attachment through and beyond their oedipal relation to their fathers.

According to this theory, boys develop an early psychic pattern of sharply defined ego boundaries and a social pattern of separation from others from this early experience of bonding and separation from their mothers. Girls learn to define themselves as continuous with others from the long attachment and merging of identity with their mothers. Their sense of self continues to be more connected to other people than is that of males. Given these differences, some of the relational differences noted in Holocaust memoirs by men and women seem explainable in terms of these cultural norms. Why else would women like Mrs. Grünwald in *Elli* and Fania Fénelon in *Playing for Time* be so absorbed in the nurturing of other women instead of concentrating exclusively on their own survival? Why do men not turn to this nurturing role as much? Why do women like Fénelon, Elli, and Gisella Perl retain their sensitivity to feelings and the suffering of others in conditions which male observers have said required the cutting off of feelings? Given the terror and unspeakable suffering of the camps, the preservation of feelings of compassion seems more remarkable than the shut-down of the emotional apparatus. But the common denominator among many male and female survivors seems to be the attempt to preserve as much of the individual's past identity as possible in the situation. This past, as we know, is different for men and women in all cultures, and Holocaust narratives demonstrate its influence upon camp prisoners. When Harsaw creates in Auschwitz a microcosm of the normal physician's world, focussing on medicines, names of diseases, and a professionally detached relationship to peers and patients, he implies a continuing standard of the past. Even in Auschwitz, he always calls everyone by his title: Dr. or Mr., never first names. Wiesel's father's detachment from other deportees, including relatives, is clearly related to his extra-familial activities and habits of his former life in Sighet. Wiesel himself, as a teenager, seems more involved in relating to others, apparently a feature of his youth.

In both cases, the determining factor is the mother, who in most societies is the primary caretaker of children. This theory removes the institution of motherhood from the realm of instinct and biological inevitability by grounding it in social relations: the experience of having been cared for by a woman creates the psychological precondition for women becoming mothers and for men to want to dominate women, who for them constitute a powerful stimulus of love and fear. Because of these relations, fathers do not "become the same kind of emotionally exclusive oedipal objects for girls that mothers do for boys" and in adulthood, "men do not become as emotionally important to women as women do to men."[41] To this one might add that males remain emotionally dependent upon females in part because they have learned to suppress dependence on other men, because they have never had a primary attachment to their own father.[42]

If women retain their ability to form empathetic friendships more often than men even in concentration and death camps, the reason may have more to do with the conditioning outlined by Chodorow than with morality, the conceptual framework adopted by many memoirists. This ability has origins, if Chodorow is right, in the oppressive situation of compulsory primary parenting by women. The purpose of this analysis is not to promote the further exploitation by women as compulsory mothers, although at first glance this oppression seems to have survival benefits in extreme situations. It makes more sense to argue that Holocaust literature makes a strong case for men to be active fathers, not only because it would free women to be more autonomous, but also because primary parenting by men would most likely enable males to develop the same capacity for friendship and empathy that women now have in greater numbers. Not only because of the next Holocaust and women's liberation, but because of the intense value now attached to world peace, the way in which human beings relate to each other has become critical. If the greater relational capacities of women could be shared by men, the world would never be the same.

Notes

1. Terrence Des Pres, *The Survivor* (New York: Oxford University Press, 1976), p. 38.

2. Estelle C. Jelinek, "Women's Autobiography and the Male Tradition," in *Women's Autobiography: Essays in Criticism*, ed. Jelinek (Bloomington: Indiana University Press, 1980), p. 10.

3. Marcus Billson and Sidonie Smith, "Lillian Hellman and the Strategy of 'Other,' " in Jelinek, *Women's Autobiography*, p. 163.

4. Alexander Donat, *The Holocaust Kingdom* (New York: Holt, Rinehart, and Winston, 1965), p. 237.

5. Germaine Tillion, *Ravensbrück* (Garden City, N.Y.: Doubleday, 1975), p. 230.

6. Hermann Langbein, *Menschen in Auschwitz* (Vienna: Europa Verlags-AG, 1972), p. 37; quoted from Benedikt Kautsky, *Teufel und Verdammte: Erfahrungen und Erkenntnisse aus sieben Jahren in deutschen Konzentrationslagern* (Vienna: Wiener Volksbuchhandlung, 1961). (My translation.)

7. Izaak Goldberg, M.D., *The Miracles Versus Tyranny* (New York: Philosophical Library, 1978).

8. Fania Fénelon, *Playing for Time*, trans. Judith Landry (New York: Atheneum, 1976), p. 155.

9. Fénelon, p. 46.

10. Ibid., p. 248.

11. Ibid., p. 131.

12. Langbein, p. 91–95; Anna Pawełczyńska, *Values and Violence in Auschwitz* (Berkeley: University of California Press, 1979), pp. 11–12, 49–50, 53, 66.

13. Fénelon, p. 106.

14. Ibid., p. 147.

15. Ibid., p. 232.

16. Fénelon with Marcelle Routier, *Sursis pour l'orchestre* (Paris: France Loisirs and Stock/Opera Mundi, 1976), pp. 311, 315–17.

17. Source of evidence for the identity of Goldberg and Harsaw is a personal letter to me, July 31, 1985.

18. Ibid., pp. 239, 243–44. A *Pfleger* tells Harsaw upon arrival that 80% of the new arrivals will die within two weeks (p. 198). Other accounts give the *maximum* time for prisoners who fail to "organize" extra food (steal from the camp) as three months.

19. In his letter of July 31, 1985, Dr. Goldberg states: "Dr. Epstein died a few years ago in Israel (Rehovoth) as a result of suffering in Auschwitz."

20. Ibid., p. 389.

21. Ibid., p. 276.

22. Ibid., p. 277.

23. Gisella Perl, *I Was a Doctor in Auschwitz* (Salem, N.H.: Ayer Company, 1984). (Originally published in 1948.)

24. Ibid., p. 75.

25. Ibid., pp. 75–76.

26. Lawrence L. Langer, *Versions of Survival* (Albany: State University of New York Press, 1982), pp. 75, 78–82.

27. Ella Lingens-Reiner, *Prisoners of Fear* (London: Victor Gollancz, 1948), p. 82.

28. Ibid., p. 83.

29. Charlotte Delbo, *None of Us Will Return*, trans. John Githens (New York: Grove Press, 1968).

30. Elie Wiesel, *Night; Dawn; The accident; Three tales* (New York: Hill and Wang, 1972); Livia E. Bitton Jackson, *Elli; Coming of Age in the Holocaust* (New York: Times Books, 1980).

31. Langbein, pp. 91–93.

32. Wiesel, p. 62.

33. Ibid., p. 75.

34. Ibid., p. 82.

35. Jackson, p. 139.

36. Tadeusz Borowski, *This Way for the Gas, Ladies and Gentlemen* (New York: Penguin, 1980).

37. Ibid., p. 48.

38. Ibid., p. 30.

39. Langer, pp. 73–74; Joan Miriam Ringelheim, "The Unethical and the Unspeakable: Women and the Holocaust," *Simon Wiesenthal Center Annual* 1 (1984), pp. 79–80.

40. Nancy Chodorow, *The Reproduction of Mothering* (Berkeley: University of California Press, 1978), pp. 199–209.

41. Ibid., p. 198.

42. Ibid., p. 176.

IV

AUTHENTICITY

From the first reports about the concentration camps in newspapers to the recent publications of the Institute for Historical Review (which say that the Holocaust never occurred or never involved gas chambers and crematoria), disbelief and denial have haunted attempts to deal with the Holocaust. As literature about recent historical events that still strongly influence the lives of many people, Holocaust narratives are read as more than imaginative literature. The statements they make about the past are judged partly on grounds of historical accuracy. Since most readers have at best a partial knowledge of the events, the credibility of Holocaust memoirs and novels is an important issue. Many events depicted in Holocaust literature seemed unbelievable to the prisoners when they were experiencing them and often still seem incredible after survival. The writer who strives to describe such events has the difficult task of evoking both the otherness of the Holocaust and its reality. To accomplish these ends, Holocaust literature must rely not only upon facts but also on such literary elements as generic devices of authenticity, characterization and dialogue, description, and the use of subjectivity. A reader's willingness to grant authenticity to Holocaust literature depends in large measure upon the skill with which a combination of literary techniques is handled, thus eliciting reader involvement and emotional response.

As in all literary works, genre is one important determinant of credibility in Holocaust narratives. Ordinarily, the memoir narrates autobiographical events in the first person and makes a claim to the actual occurrence of the events in the past. It is a more outward-directed form than the autobiography proper, describing the people and events known to the author more than interior development.[1] In contrast, the novel claims to be more or less completely imagined, even if it includes a variety of historical data or backgrounds. However, Holocaust literature tends to obscure the boundary between factual and fictional forms because many writers feel compelled to make imagination serve fact rather than the reverse. "For when fact itself surpasses fiction, what is there left for the novel and short story to do?" asks Alvin Rosenfeld.[2] Imagination tends to be used to provide a narrative perspective and to make the facts, which are often difficult enough to take in, more accessible to the senses. Thus, memoirs often have the look and density of fiction. Conversely, while fiction may serve to create a representative version or a specific perspective of the Holocaust, it often tends to borrow autobiographical or documentary conventions to extend its credibility. While some Holocaust novels do alter historical facts, such works do not fare well with the critics and others who know what is being changed. Some examples will be discussed below.

For the Holocaust memoir to make its claim to refer to real events, it must employ certain strategies to convince the reader that it is more than historical prose fiction. While it usually exploits a first-person narrator, this is an insufficient distinguishing mark since many novels use the same strategy, basing their credibility upon a resemblance to eyewitness reports or memoirs. Paul Fussell has asserted, with reference to World War I novels, "the impossibility of ever satisfactorily distinguishing a memoir from a first-person novel" because the memoir is also a "kind of fiction," distinguished from the latter primarily in its "continuous implicit attestations of veracity or appeals to documented fact."[3] However, it is possible to discern authenticating devices in Holocaust texts which signal, with a fairly high degree of credibility, that the text is a memoir. These tend to be in the form of information preceding or following the text, attributed

to either the author or another person. Charlotte Delbo appends
a short biographical sketch to the end of her memoir with the
statement that she is no longer certain that what she has written
is true, but that she is sure it was faithfully recorded.[4] Fania
Fénelon precedes her memoir with a preface by Marcelle Routier,
her co-author, which presents the surviving members of the
orchestra in the present and Fénelon as the chief informant.
(The exact amount of Fénelon's cooperation with Routier remains nebulous, a factor which detracts from the credibility
somewhat.) In the original French version, *Sursis pour l'orchestre,*
an organizational chart of the orchestra members and a diagram
of the music barracks add to the impression of documentation.
Dribben employs the device of a foreword by a famous person,
Golda Meir, who assures the reader that the text represents not
only the "largely autobiographical . . . stages of an extraordinary
life, but the stages of the history of her people."[5] Since Dribben
claims to be an exceptional heroine, the confirmation of her
importance by a national leader is appropriate. Nevertheless,
the word "largely" before autobiographical does little to resolve
the entangling of fact and fiction in the text. A more immediately
convincing way to refer to real events is the use of photographs
of family members described in the text. Both Judith Dribben
and Gerda Klein authenticate their memoirs in this way. Klein
and Livia Bitton Jackson include dedications and acknowledg-
ments which refer to persons described in their memoirs or
others who assisted in the project of remembering.

Novels lack such references to reality actually experienced by
the author. Instead, they exploit other "realistic" conventions,
such as names of specific places and persons taken from the
history of the Holocaust, as well as representative events such
as confinements to ghettos and deportation. These references
to historical reality are numerous and specific in *Anya,* unlike
Ilse Aichinger's *Herod's Children.* The latter symbolic novel includes only enough historical references to suggest a Nazi-oc-
cupied city, but not the name of the setting, the date of the
events, or the name of the oppressors other than "Secret Police."
This technique serves the author's end of universalizing history
to convey a symbolic, religious meaning which transcends the
specifics of time and place.

The majority of narrative strategies in *Anya* signal that, however convincing, it is fiction. These include the fact that author and protagonist have different names, the subtitle "a novel" on the title page, and the publisher's diction at the beginning and on the back cover. The most trustworthy of these devices is the word "novel"; the rest are conventions which have also been used in autobiographical works.[6] A major authenticating device of this novel is its imitation of a memoir through the first-person narrator, who relates her memories of the collision of her life with the Holocaust. In addition to this fictional strategy, several of the novel's divisions are preceded by Russian fables which an implied authorial voice attributes to "Anya Savikin" or "Mrs. Anya Meyers" (her second married name). This claim of an informant by the author's presumed voice is like the prefaces and photographs in a memoir which direct one toward a point of reference outside the text. In *Anya*, the claim of an informant is subordinated to the fictional devices and signals and by itself is insufficient proof of an outside informant. This evidence can be found outside the text, in Harold Ribalow's *The Tie That Binds*, where an interview with Susan Fromberg Schaeffer indicates that the novel is based primarily upon interviews with one real survivor.[7] This partly explains how the author, not personally involved in the Holocaust, became well-enough informed to adopt the persona of a survivor. However, the basis in fact could also be derived from reading real memoirs. In any case, the novel by itself is meant to be read as fiction.

If we disregard all extraneous criteria, the primary difference between claims to authenticity of novels and memoirs is that of reference to the actual experience of the author in memoirs and the general lack of this reference in the novels. While each of the memoirs refers to the real experience of the author, they are far from equal in the impression of credibility which they make. Some of these memoirs seem much less credible than the novel *Anya*, because genre is only one among a whole series of criteria which contribute to authenticity in Holocaust texts: characterization, perspective, description, and their relation to factual truth.

Characterization in memoirs and novels about the Holocaust plays an important role in the creation of a credible vision. The protagonists in Schaeffer, Delbo, and Klein, who tend to minimize their own survival actions and displays of courage, are more easily credible survivor characters than those of Dribben or Fénelon. The survivors in Schaeffer, Delbo, and Klein tend to reflect the powerlessness and suffering of Jewish and other prisoners, thus better reflecting the actual negativity and destructive aspects of the ordeal than the character who represents an ideal of resistance, as is more common in Dribben and Fénelon. Jackson's self-portrayal occupies a middle ground, combining the aims of conveying the torments more realistically (partly because Jackson's position in the camps is more ordinary than Dribben's or Fénelon's) as well as the moments of transcendence and resistance. However, each of these writers must also deal with the conflicting demands of portraying the actual brutality but not appearing to suffer excessively. At times, feelings of guilt counteract the urge to show the full horror of the atrocities through their effect on the survivor. Many Holocaust memoirists, according to Hamida Bosmajian, "dwell little on their personal, physical, and mental agonies . . . because dwelling on such suffering would make the autobiographer guilty against those who succumbed."[8] As we have seen in Chapter II, Schaeffer detaches herself from her suffering by means of humor and distracting images, while Klein describes her suffering with a restained, unemotional style. Both texts imply that the process of memory has selected part of the reality to reveal and has left out other parts which were either too painful to remember or depart too far from the author's world view. (The latter seems especially true for Klein.) Because the narrators do not conceal the role of subjective recall, the texts retain their authenticity as memoirs, although the reader must be alert to the fact that the texts do not pretend to give a full picture of Holocaust atrocities or negativity. A critic such as Alan Mintz, who judges *Anya* in terms of a standard of realism by which it was never meant to be measured, condemns it for its overemphasis on dialogue in domestic interiors, which, while constituting pockets of resistance in a brutal world, also indicates an "inability or unwillingness to imagine the gigantic external scale of the Nazi murder of the Jews."[9] The screening out of radical evil is not a consequence of the "universalist perspective" as Mintz suggests, but of a literary strategy based upon memory and attachments to people who have perished. William Novak's insight into *Anya* comes closer to the truth:

It is not directly about the holocaust so much as the period in which the holocaust occurred, and the personal history with which it intersects. This is not a book about suffering nor about the horrors of the holocaust; its substance is rather fictionalized memory which seeks to dwell on human goodness more than on depravity and evil.[10]

Of the four memoirs, Gerda Klein shares the tendency of this novel "to dwell on human goodness." The other three resolve the problem of how to portray suffering and evil in different ways.

Delbo avoids the emphasis upon personal suffering at the expense of the non-survivors by stressing collective suffering. Her technique of using primarily the first-person plural as a lyrical voice allows her to subsume her personal suffering into the collective. This collective portrait enables her to emphasize atrocity and suffering to a far greater degree than the other self-effacing writers without disrupting the bond of equality between herself as survivor and the dead.

In Schaeffer and Delbo, the self-effacing protagonist tends to account for survival by referring to impersonal forces beyond the control of self, thus discounting the importance of individual action. Since such actions often did not prevent people from escaping their fate, the role of personal initiative appears negligible in these accounts. Such survival narratives highlight other factors instead: the role of coincidence and chance (in *Anya*), the inexplicable resources of hidden physical endurance (in Delbo), and the importance of the assistance of others. The psychological realism of emphasizing these factors is greater than a characterization which over-emphasizes the significance of individual action. In Klein, Schaeffer, and Delbo, the additional need to canonize the dead prisoners who were not properly mourned before is a contributing factor in the self-effacing self-portrayal.

Most of the self-dramatizing characterizations go much further than Schaeffer, Delbo, or Klein in obscuring the suffering of the Holocaust victim. Although parts of these texts document familiar Holocaust terrain and events with some objectivity, this mode of character portrayal seems to respond primarily to a post-Holocaust need by the survivor to idealize the self in terms of resistance. Although the need to cast the self in a heroic pose is as psychologically real as the need to magnify the heroic actions of someone else, the impression of authenticity is less in the self-dramatizing portrayals. The emphasis upon the individual's battle against Nazi officials for the purpose of demonstrating victories tends to magnify the moral courage of a single individual while obscuring the interdependence of all victims, the powerlessness of most of them, and the limitation of collective punishment, as well as the role of privileged status and chance. The demonstration of resistance victories depends frequently upon dramatic shows of angry rhetoric and a concealment of personal vulnerability. When vulnerability and suffering are denied too much, as in Dribben, the characterization loses much credibility. Occasionally Dribben admits to feeling afraid or demoralized, but not enough to be convincing.

Dribben's self-dramatizing portrayal tends to conceal her problematic relationship to those less fortunate. She does not deal convincingly with her privileged position and the accompanying moral ambiguity.

Although the self-dramatizing style of *Playing for Time* presents some problems of authenticity, Fénelon's characterization is much more credible than that of Dribben. While the governing idea of the narrator's exemplary resistance sometimes leads to excessive claims of virtue in contrast to the supposed selfishness of the other orchestra members, Fénelon's self-portrait includes some admissions of guilt for the moral ambivalence of her position as one of the Birkenau elite. In addition, she acknowledges her position as singer and orchestrator as the source of some of her resistance possibilities. She maximizes her moments of defiance but does not entirely obscure her vulnerability to the whims of the SS and her own desire to survive.

Fénelon undercuts her own self-dramatizing tendencies at times through humor and detachment from her own self-importance. For example, she describes her performance as a drummer in one of the Birkenau concerts as a grotesque comedy after having to learn the skill in one week to replace a sick player. The narrator's emphasis upon her ridiculous appearance in performing the marathon demanded by the *Lagerführerin* has a muting effect upon her self-idealization and increases the authenticity.

Jackson's approach is authentic because her riskier actions are psychologically motivated by the need to save or help her mother. Her claim of a superior awareness of events is an ability to see the Nazi net closing around the Hungarians and to express the truth without illusions. But it has limitations which she also acknowledges: late in the book, she admits that she still hopes to find all their family members and relatives alive after the war, and her brother must disillusion her.[11] She admits that despite knowing about the gas chambers, she had stubbornly clung to the myth of the camp for the elderly and children and had not fully believed in the murder of women with their children. Her inconsistency in this matter seems credible as evidence that the need to hope for a reunion with loved ones often supersedes the pose of superior clear-sightedness.

In general, the self-dramatizing style tends to seem more artificial than the self-effacing style, but the credibility varies depending upon the inclusion of more vulnerable and realistic aspects of the portrayal. Other factors which may affect credibility include recognition of privilege as one basis for resistance poses, explicit references to suffering and fear, and skill in reproducing speech and dialogue.

The significance of skillfully written dialogue tends to be greater among the self-dramatizing writers and in *Anya,* where it is used more extensively than in Klein or Delbo. In Dribben, the frequently wooden quality of the speech adds difficulty to believing the claims of the protagonist, which are in themselves quite exceptional. For example, Dribben, almost dying in the Birkenau infirmary, says to her friend, "No, don't weep Laura. I will not die. . . . Oh, I will not die, but Laura, if I lie in back of the partition, will you come and see me?"[12] There may be reasons other than inauthenticity for the author's avoidance cf contractions, inappropriate interjections ("Oh, I will not die,"), and choppy, short sentences. Whatever Dribben's skill in writing in other languages, she lacks native familiarity with English. Since she is a professional translator, one would expect her writing ability in English to be better.[13] Sometimes the speech is better written than this quotation, but it is rarely distinctively natural.

Both Fénelon and Jackson employ speech which enhances the authenticity of their characterizations. Most of the speech in Fénelon is directed to other members of the orchestra, while expressions of resistance to the SS are much more covert. This is a naturalistic element increasing credibility over Dribben. Fénelon's occasional speech to the SS tends to be correct, standard French, while her remarks to the other musicians tend to be more informal. The colloquial and vulgar speech conveys not only credible information about the origin of the speaker, but a great deal of hostility which has few other vents.

While the dialogue in Jackson's *Elli* is simple and effective, the author's greatest success is in her imitation of the consciousness and emotional outbursts of herself as a thirteen-year-old. Elli's thinking as well as speech often is rendered as interior monologue. Many events of the camps and deportation process acquire a fresh immediacy through this hyperbolic language. For example, Elli's shock upon seeing menstrual blood on the inside of a woman's legs at roll call is expressed with the impetuousness of the teenager, strangely ironic in this setting: "I would rather die than have blood flowing down my legs." Her susceptibility to feeling embarrassment more intensely than an adult also brings the dehumanization of the boxcar ride into sharp focus: "It is inconceivable for me to use the pot in public."[14] The narrative perspective of a teenaged girl who habitually reacts with naiveté, intense feeling, and intelligence conveys credibly the possibility of a child surviving Auschwitz with her essential humanity intact.

The natural-sounding dialogue in *Anya* is an important feature since the novel cannot depend upon the same expectations of truth which surround the memoir or the fictional creation of a survivor. The enormous quantity of direct speech in the novel places a large burden upon the considerable skill of the author. Direct speech conveys both the anger and suffering of the survivor and her ability to take advantage of circumstance for her survival. For example, Anya saves herself from a threatening interrogator by intercepting another officer:

"Oh, Sir," I babbled in Polish, "I've been accused falsely, just because I wouldn't go out with him; he gave me cod liver oil and a white uniform. I didn't do anything, believe me, I didn't do anything; I re-

member you from Warsaw, I'm Polish," I babbled, " I don't speak a
word of German."[15]

This quotation shows the chaotic, incoherent state of the protagonist's mind through the non-chronological sequence of information, of which the oil and uniform is gratuitous, as well
as the self-effacing evaluation by the present-time narrator of
her speech as "babble." Despite the lack of chronological co-
herence, the sentence includes all the information necessary for
the protagonist to get herself saved, yet without much self-idealization. It is typical of the self-portrait of the fictional narrator.

Dialogue and speech are much less important in Delbo and
Klein. One of the more credible aspects of the two memoirs is
the way minimal amounts of speech convey the extremity of the
conditions described. Although both Klein and Delbo assert the
importance of conversation for maintaining morale, they do not
include very much direct speech. They emphasize instances in
which silence prevails as indications of excessive suffering or
emotion. These memoirs also employ other narrative strategies
for credibility which are more important than speech. In general,
direct discourse is an element which may contribute to the credibility or its lack in certain texts, but not always. Its most positive
impact can be seen in Schaeffer and its most negative impact in
Dribben, since in both of these it constitutes the bulk of the
narrative.

Another traditional technique of realistic fiction, objective description, is employed by Schaeffer, Dribben, and Klein. The
authenticity conveyed by such attempts at objectivity is that of
approximating documentation or *reportage* within a semi-fictional
text. The recurrence of similar persons or phenomena in such
documentary passages in various texts tends to authenticate an
individual text. However, objectivity by itself tends to be inadequate in a Holocaust memoir because the subject matter ex-
poses the illusory quality of impartiality. Excessive objectivity
may indicate the hiding of feelings and subjectivity rather than
scientific truth. The "objectivity" of description in Dribben conceals most feelings associated with suffering while claiming the
factuality of heroic actions. The realistic illusion breaks down
because the rationality does not fit the circumstances except in

the enumeration of familiar features of Birkenau. Especially when objective description narrates hard work or beatings inflicted on the narrator, the illusion is incomplete because the suppression of feelings is obvious.

In several memoirs, the display of a relationship between risk and strong bonding between survivor characters adds to the credibility of such risks taken. For example, Gerda Klein's life is saved while she is undergoing slow death in a punishment work group at Märzdorf because of a combination of coincidental factors and her friend's risk. The arrival of her former camp director looking for trained weavers is highly coincidental. Ilse's presence in the flax detail on the same day is also the result of chance. However, her decision to accompany her friend and her stratagem of making Gerda raise her arm when Ilse's number is called out, and then begging for her own release from Märzdorf, are credible manifestations of the emotional interdependence of female friends. Klein does not explicitly state that Ilse believes their survival to be linked, but Klein reveals elsewhere that she has the power to change Ilse's moods and consistently conveys that they are inseparable. Thus, the risk has a basis in need, and its probability increases. In a similar but more explicit fashion, Jackson motivates Elli's confrontations with the SS in Auschwitz by her attachment to her mother. The fact that Jackson is remembering herself rather than a friend gives her the possibility of revealing her own motives, whereas Klein only hints at those of Ilse. Similar incentives for risky confrontations are implicit in Schaeffer's novel *Anya*. As a result, these actions seem less derived from present-day concerns about resistance than those in Dribben or Fénelon. In the latter works, the few somewhat abstracted descriptions of friendships increase the believability of some of the resistance actions.

Anya is another example of the complementary techniques of realism and expressions of feeling through imagery and dialogue. A wealth of details recreates bourgeois life in prewar Poland and the substance of the Holocaust experience of the protagonist. Her inner life is revealed not only in terms of thoughts and dream images, but also in her role as narrator supplying poetic similes and metaphors which concretize the described reality in terms of familiar images. Thus Anya's expressions tend to engage the reader's imaginative participation. For example, "His skull shattered like an egg" and "I sat on the valise like a hen hatching a crocodile" familiarize the unfamiliar and do much to increase the reader's ability to participate imaginatively in the events.[16] The power of the familiar and ingenious analogies overcomes the artificiality of the narrator's language.

In their own ways, Delbo and Fénelon use strategies based upon a heightening of the subjective to persuade the reader of their authenticity. The lyrical prose of Delbo conveys the otherworldly atmosphere of Birkenau in surrealistic images from which most other frames of reference have disappeared. Images of bodies which have been transformed into visual cries or blocks of ice carry a large weight of feeling and perception. The reader experiences the self-contained world of pain to an extent unrivaled by the other texts. The repetition of the same phrases in succeeding sentences which are varied enough to avoid excessive monotony evokes the long duration of pain by making the reader participate in its long continuity. The combination of a variety of typical scenes of suffering in Birkenau and the evocative, lyrical strategies creates one of the most credible Holocaust texts.

What is nearer to eternity than a day? What is longer than a day? How can one know that it is passing? Clod follows clod, the furrow moves back, the carriers continue their rounds. And screams, screams, screams. What is longer than a day? Time passes because the fog slowly lifts. [17]

Fénelon's *Playing for Time*, a memoir with a claim to documentary truth and a somewhat realistic technique, also employs a narrative technique of emotionally loaded language to communicate the subjective perspective and anger of the narrator. This sharp anger and the use of vivid metaphorical images draw the reader into the narrator's experience more fully than objective description. Her colorful descriptions of the *kapos* and the SS are convincing because the exaggerations reflect the emotional reality of her position. However, this outward expression of anger is a phenomenon of the survivor after liberation, not during the event itself. As Fénelon suggests, the inmates had to refrain from showing their real feelings to their masters. For example, her description of Commandant Kramer, weeping over music after shattering women's skulls, or her views of the Polish "Aryans" as uncivilized, grotesque giants, are verbal acts of revenge. Fénelon's satirical techniques create a credible perspective for glimpses of the oppressors in the orchestra. Her mixture of objective description and emotion is more credible than a purely abstract objectivity since it incorporates a credible observer perspective.

The scarcity of hostility or selfish behavior among the inmates in many of the memoirs is an aspect of the memoirist's tendency to limit the portrayal of evil, especially the manifestation of the system in inmate relations. Only Fénelon among the women's texts surveyed makes egocentrism an important issue. Authors such as Klein, Schaeffer, and Jackson focus narrowly on the fate of the narrator and a few friends or family members, where support and sharing are most plausible. However, the inclusion of at least some evidence of conflict and selfishness in Schaeffer and Jackson's narratives increases their value as representative documents. The novel has very little if any "objective description" and relies largely upon symbolism, lyrical narrative, and dialogue for its imaginative vision.

Facts and Authenticity

Because Holocaust literature is, for the present, inevitably judged in part by documentary criteria, the question of factual truth must be considered. Such media events as the television docudrama "Holocaust" and the film "Seven Beauties" by Lina Wertmüller attracted intense controversy largely because of their departures from fact in combination with popular success and a wide impact. Erich Dorf, the fictitious Nazi in "Holocaust" who directs everything from *Kristallnacht* to Auschwitz, conceals the bureaucratization of genocide which made possible the division of responsibility *ad infinitum*. Bruno Bettelheim and Alvin Rosenfeld have criticized the portrayal of a female camp commandant, which contradicts the Nazi view of women in the film "Seven Beauties." When significant facts about Holocaust reality are changed by an artist for purely aesthetic or sensational ends, the critical evaluation of a particular work will be negatively affected. However, the work may be valuable for its impact on other grounds. As Andreas Huyssen points out in his essay on the docudrama "Holocaust," the emotional impact of the series in West Germany was greater on the public than any of the factually correct or aesthetically better artistic versions of the Holocaust.[18] The emotional impact and the possibility of identification may be most important for the impact of a dramatic or fictional work, but it may still present an ethical problem: the dissemination and popularization of historical inaccuracies and the skepticism of some educated segments of the public.

The importance of factual accuracy is neither fixed nor uniform in a particular work. Some facts are more important than others in a Holocaust work, depending upon whether they are intrinsic to the Holocaust experience, or related to contextual matters. Sidra Ezrahi has criticized *Anya* for its lack of accuracy with regard to Hasidic life despite its correctness in most other respects.[19] Although someone who knows a good deal about Hasidic life will find such lapses more serious than other readers, such omissions seem objectively less significant than omissions of suffering and physical brutality in Aichinger or conflict in Klein.

The credibility of memoirs depends to a considerable extent upon the reliability of the author's memory. Consequently, the date of composition has some bearing upon the claim that the memories are authentic. A memoir written in 1945 or 1950 will more likely be based upon vivid and precise memories than one written in 1970 or 1980, other things being equal. Sometimes the date of composition precedes the date of publication by many years, such as Charlotte Delbo's *None of Us Will Return*, written in 1945 but published in 1965, and Izaak Goldberg's *The Miracles Versus Tyranny*, which was written immediately after the war, according to the preface, although published in 1978. Such a claim, together with detailed descriptions, adds credence to the work.

The women's memoirs which have the earliest dates of composition in this study are *None of Us Will Return* by Charlotte Delbo (1945), *I Was a Doctor in Auschwitz* by Gisela Perl (1948), and *All But My Life* by Gerda Klein (1957). The relatively early dates of composition, particularly for Delbo and Perl, reinforce the believability of the memories, such as the claims for inmate bonding and assistance. The more recent memoirs, Dribben's *A Girl Called Judith Strick* (1970), Fénelon's *Playing for Time* (1977), and Jackson's *Elli* (1980) must depend more upon fictional techniques, plausible narratives, and confirmation by other testimonies. Especially when these narratives make great claims for resistance actions, the recent dates of publication and composition tend to diminish the likelihood of complete factuality.

The validity of a given survival narrative depends in part upon the writer's fidelity to distinctions among types of concentration camps, which have been discussed by many scholars and others.[20] The distinctions indicate tendencies rather than fixed categories. In general, conditions in labor camps were better than those in death camps; there were fewer selections, less overcrowding, better food rations, less brutality and strict control. However, the distinctions were often blurred because of changes in conditions at different times and variations in the Nazis' intentions with regard to inmates (i.e., killing versus cheap labor). Schaeffer in *Anya* and Klein in *All But My Life* both deal with a labor camp experience and portray relatively better conditions. Anya's successful escape, the relative lack of overcrowding in both texts, and Klein's theatrical performances would be far less credible in texts about a death camp. However, the conditions of the death march in Klein show that the experiences of a labor camp inmate could change drastically.

However, the kind of camp described is not always the most important fact in accounting for the way inmates are treated in a Holocaust text. Delbo, Dribben, and Fénelon all portray life and death in Birkenau, the women's camp of Auschwitz, a major center of Nazi destruction. The degree of suffering and the possibilities for transcendence differ considerably, based in part upon the status of the prisoner in the camp hierarchy. Delbo, a French political prisoner, portrays Birkenau as relentless pain which she and a mass of others endure; Dribben portrays Birkenau as a place where much suffering could be avoided through special status, disguise, and solidarity; while Fénelon portrays the suffering of the ordinary prisoners from the greatest distance, since she is the most protected through position of all three survivors except for the earliest and latter stages of confinement. The view of Birkenau, therefore, depends in large part upon the narrator's position in the camp hierarchy. This is even more significant than ethnic or national category, even though each of the texts refers to the greater violence and more frequent selections against Jews. Delbo, a non-Jewish political prisoner, contributes the most negative vision of a death camp, while Dribben and Fénelon, to varying degrees self-identified as Jewish, moderate their views of camp suffering with personal self-portraits of self-dramatizing resistance. Thus, in this respect, the author's ethnic vulnerability is less important to the kind of view of camp suffering than the type of resistance image which the Jewish author endeavors to convey. Elements of this type of portrayal have also been described in Klein, a Jewish survivor, who restricts the amount of negativity in part by showing personal successes. The tendency of Jewish authors to write more optimistically of the Holocaust than non-Jews has been noted by Edith Naveh Brown in her dissertation, "Dramaturgical Problems in Plays with the Theme of the Nazi Holocaust."[21] The sample of these two studies is too small to provide a conclusive answer, but it may indicate a trend that would have logical reasons, i.e., the desire of many Jews to redeem the image of the victims of the Holocaust who were said to have gone to the slaughter like sheep.[22]

In conclusion, what we have distilled from the texts studied here as authenticating devices are a variety of conventional literary strategies which acquire more importance in dealing with the material in such texts than in more customary literary works. In addition, the omission or manipulation of aspects of the typical ghetto or camp experience may be a serious flaw. The judging of whether facts are true or not may be a particularly vexing problem, since the Nazis applied many of their policies inconsistently and arbitrarily. The role of genre is never more than a matter of faith, but the problems of distinguishing fictional and factual forms in Holocaust literature require much more than a recognition of conventional signs. A variety of authenticating devices and factors exist in interrelationship, from external issues like the author's relationship to actual history to the various literary techniques and the completeness of the reality portrayed. While literary evaluation is particularly difficult for Holocaust texts, it would be untrue to say that all are equally compelling or that the question of quality is unimportant. If the point is for more people to read these books, the critic will have to confront the issue of why people will benefit from certain texts and not others. The case of the televised program "Holocaust" illustrates the importance of identification with the characters which may outweigh the flaws in facts or artistry. The critic will never be able to unearth all the important factors which make a given text compelling to an audience, since many of these will be located in the psychology of the audience rather than in the text or work itself.

The authenticity of the texts studied stems first from the power of the writing to engage the emotions and imagination, and second from a consideration of factual consistency. Three of the six texts succeed more than the others in terms of emotional engagement of the reader and documentary truth. These are Charlotte Delbo's *None of Us Will Return*, Susan Schaeffer's *Anya*, and Livia Jackson's *Elli*. The ability of these texts to capture the experience of victimization is dependent upon a lyrical use of prose which surpasses the other texts. This conclusion seems to agree with that of Alvin Rosenfeld, who remarks that Holocaust fiction is

often most memorable when it departs from the traditional ways of the novel and begins to approach the condition of poetry. What lingers on frequently has less to do with the narrative elements of plot development and character portrayal than with the presentation of feeling through certain brilliant images.[23]

However, what is memorable and what is authentic may not always be identical. The human desire for a more heroic transcendence of adversity may contribute to an acceptance of Dribben and Fénelon, and the need for female heroes by female readers may increase the acceptability of these authors. Since this literature is not pure myth, however, credibility even for hero-seekers eventually must take into consideration the extreme obstacles to survival and resistance or else forfeit its claims to heroism.

Notes

1. M. H. Abrams, *A Glossary of Literary Terms*, 4th ed. (New York: Holt, Rinehart and Winston, 1981), p. 15.

2. Alvin H. Rosenfeld, *A Double Dying* (Bloomington: Indiana University Press, 1980), p. 65.

3. Paul Fussell, *The Great War and Modern Memory* (New York: Oxford University Press, 1975), p. 310.

4. Charlotte Delbo, *None of Us Will Return* (New York: Grove Press, 1968).

5. Judith Dribben, *A Girl Called Judith Strick* (New York: Cowles Book Company, 1970).

6. William C. Spengemann, *The Forms of Autobiography: Episodes in the History of the Literary Genre* (New Haven: Yale University Press, 1980), p. 119.

7. Harold U. Ribalow, *The Tie That Binds: Conversations with Jewish Writers* (San Diego: A. S. Barnes, 1980), pp. 77–92.

8. Hamida Bosmajian, *Metaphors of Evil: Contemporary German Literature and the Shadow of Nazism* (Iowa City: University of Iowa Press, 1979), p. 35.

9. Alan Mintz, "Mothers and Daughters," *Commentary* 59 (March, 1975), p. 90.

10. William Novak, "Anya," *New York Times Book Review*, October 20, 1974, p. 36.

11. Livia Bitton Jackson, *Elli: Coming of Age in the Holocaust* (New York: Times Books, 1980), pp. 176–77.

12. Dribben, pp. 210–11.

13. Biographical data in *Contemporary Authors* 37–40, 1st rev. ed. (Detroit: Gale Research, 1979), p. 142.

14. Jackson, p. 65.

15. Susan Fromberg Schaeffer, *Anya* (New York: Avon Books, 1974), p. 398.

16. Ibid., pp. 596, 459.

17. Delbo, p. 54.

18. Andreas Huyssen, "The Politics of Identification," *New German Critique* 19 (Winter, 1980): 117–36, especially 121–22.

19. Sidra Ezrahi, *By Words Alone: The Holocaust in Literature* (Chicago: The University of Chicago Press, 1980), p. 215.

20. Eugen Kogon, *The Theory and Practice of Hell* (New York: Octagon-Farrar, Straus and Giroux, 1973), pp. 35–36; Terrence Des Pres, *The Survivor: An Anatomy of Life in the Death Camps* (New York: Oxford University Press, 1976).

21. Edith Brown Naveh, "Dramaturgical Problems in Plays with the Theme of the Nazi Holocaust," Diss. University of Pittsburgh, 1977, p. 242.

22. Alexander discusses this desire and its reflection in Israeli literature in *The Resonance of Dust: Essays on Holocaust Literature and Jewish Fate* (Columbus: Ohio State University Press, 1979), pp. 73–118.

23. Rosenfeld, p. 169.

BIBLIOGRAPHY

Fiction, Memoirs, and Collected Testimonies

Aichinger, Ilse. *Herod's Children.* Trans. Cornelia Schaeffer. New York: Atheneum, 1963.

———. *Die grössere Hoffnung.* 1st ed. Amsterdam: Bermann-Fischer, 1948; 2nd ed. Frankfurt a.M.: S. Fischer, 1960.

Alton (Tauber), Ruth. *Deportiert von den Nazis.* unpub. ms., Leo Baeck Institute. 1961, based on 1945 report.

Améry, Jean. *At the Mind's Limits: Contemplations By a Survivor on Auschwitz and Its Realities.* Trans. Sidney Rosenfeld and Stella P. Rosenfeld. Bloomington: Indiana University Press, 1980.

Apenszlak, Jacob, ed. *The Black Book of Polish Jewry.* New York: Roy Publishers, 1943.

Berger, Zdena. *Tell Me Another Morning.* New York: Harper and Brothers, 1959.

Birenbaum, Halina. *Hope is the Last to Die.* Trans. David Welsh. New York: Twayne, 1971.

Borowski, Tadeusz. *This Way for the Gas, Ladies and Gentlemen.* Trans. Barbara Vedder. New York: Penguin, 1980.

Buber, Margarete. *Als Gefangene bei Stalin und Hitler.* Munich: Verlag der Zwölf, c. 1949.

———. *Mistress to Kafka: The Life and Death of Milena.* London: Secker and Warburg, 1966.

———. *Under Two Dictators.* Trans. Edward Fitzgerald. New York: Dodd, Mead, and Company, 1949.

Delbo, Charlotte. *Aucun de nous ne reviendra.* Paris: Gonthier, 1965.

————. *Une connaissance inutile.* Paris: Éditions de Minuit, 1970.

————. *Le convoi du 24. janvier.* Paris: Éditions de Minuit, 1965.

————. *La mémoire et les jours.* Paris: Éditions Berg International, 1985.

————. *Mesure de nos jours.* Paris: Éditions de Minuit, 1971.

————. *None of Us Will Return.* Trans. John Githens. New York: Grove Press, 1968.

————. "Phantoms, My Companions." Trans. Rosette C. Lamont. *The Massachusetts Review* XII, no. 1 (Winter, 1971): 10–31.

————. *Qui rapportera ces paroles?* Paris: Harmattan, 1974.

————. *Spectres, mes compagnons.* Lausanne: M. Bridel, 1977.

————."Who Will Carry the Word?" in Robert Skloot, ed. *The Theatre of the Holocaust; Four Plays.* Madison: The University of Wisconsin Press, 1982.

Donat, Alexander. *The Holocaust Kingdom.* New York: Holt, Rinehart, and Winston, 1965.

Dribben, Judith. *And Some Shall Live.* Jerusalem: Keter Books, 1969.

————. *A Girl Called Judith Strick.* New York: Cowles Book Company, 1970.

Eliach, Yaffa. *Hasidic Tales of the Holocaust.* New York: Oxford University Press, 1982.

Fénelon, Fania. *Playing for Time.* Trans. Judith Landry. New York: Atheneum, 1977.

————, with Marcelle Routier. *Sursis pour l'orchestre.* Paris: France Loisirs and Stock/ Opera Mundi, 1976.

Frank, Anne. *The Works of Anne Frank.* Westport, Conn.: Greenwood Press, 1974.

German Women Writers of the Twentieth Century. Eds. Elizabeth Rutschi Herrmann and Edna Huttenmaier Spitz. New York: Pergamon Press, 1978.

Goldberg, Izaak. *The Miracles Versus Tyranny.* New York: Philosophical Library, 1978.

Gurdus, Luba K. *The Death Train.* New York: Schocken, 1979.

Heimler, Eugen. *Night of the Mist.* Trans. André Ungar. Westport, Conn.: Greenwood Press, 1978.

Hitler, Adolf. *Mein Kampf.* Trans. Ralph Mannheim. Boston: Houghton Mifflin Company, 1943.

Jackson, Livia Bitton. *Elli.* New York: Times Books, 1980.

Karmel, Ilona. *An Estate of Memory.* Boston: Houghton Mifflin, 1969.

Katz, Esther, and Ringelheim, Joan Miriam. *Proceedings of the Conference Women Surviving the Holocaust.* New York: The Institute for Research in History, 1983.

Ka-Tzetnik 135633. *House of Dolls.* Trans. Moshe M. Kohn. London: Frederick Muller Ltd., 1956.

Kautsky, Benedikt. *Teufel und Verdammte: Erfahrungen und Erkenntnisse aus sieben Jahren in deutschen Konzentrationslagern*. Vienna: Wiener Volksbuchhandlung, 1961.

Klein, Gerda. *All But My Life*. New York: Hill and Wang, 1957.

———. *Promise of a New Spring. The Holocaust and Renewal*. Chappaqua, N.Y.: Rossel Books, 1981.

Kogon, Eugen. *The Theory and Practice of Hell*. New York: Octagon-Farrar, Straus and Giroux, 1973.

Langbein, Hermann. *Menschen in Auschwitz*. Vienna: Europa Verlags-AG, 1972.

Langfus, Anna. *Les bagages de sable*. Paris: Gallimard, 1962.

———. *The Lost Shore*. Trans. Peter Wiles. New York: Pantheon, 1963.

———. *Le sel et le souffre*. Paris: Gallimard, 1960.

———. *The Whole Land Brimstone*. Trans. Peter Wiles. New York: Pantheon, 1963.

Laska, Vera. *Women in the Resistance and in the Holocaust*. Westport, Conn.: Greenwood Press, 1983.

Leitner, Isabella. *Fragments of Isabella: A Memoir of Auschwitz*. Ed. Irving A. Leitner. New York: T. Y. Crowell, 1978.

Lengyel, Olga. *Five Chimneys: The Story of Auschwitz*. Chicago: Ziff-Davis, 1947.

Levi, Primo. *If This is a Man*. Trans. Stuart Woolf. London: The Bodley Head-Orion Press, 1966.

Lévy-Hass, Hanna. *Inside Belsen*. Trans. Ronald Taylor. Great Britain and New Jersey: The Harvester Press and Barnes and Noble, 1982.

———. *Vielleicht war das alles erst der Anfang*. Berlin: Rotbuch Verlag, 1979.

Lifton, Robert J. *Death in Life: Survivors of Hiroshima*. New York: Vintage, 1967.

Lingens-Reiner, Ella. *Prisoners of Fear*. London: Victor Gollancz, 1948.

Meed, Vladka. *On Both Sides of the Wall: Memoirs of the Warsaw Ghetto*. Trans. M. Spiegel and S. Mead. Haifa: Ghetto Fighters House, 1972.

Morante, Elsa. *History A Novel*. Trans. William Weaver. New York: Avon Books, 1977.

Newman, Judith Sternberg. *In the Hell of Auschwitz*. New York: Exposition. 1964.

Perl, Gisella. *I Was a Doctor in Auschwitz*. Salem, N.H.: Ayer Company, 1984.

Rosen, Norma. *Touching Evil*. New York: Harcourt, Brace, and World, 1969.

Rousset, David. *L'univers concentrationnaire*. New York: Reynal and Hitchcock, 1947.

———. *The Other Kingdom*. Trans. Ramon Guthrie. New York: Howard Fertig, 1982.

Sachs, Nelly. *O the Chimneys*. Trans. Michael Hamburger et. al. New York: Farrar, Straus and Giroux, 1967.

———. *Zeichen im Sand. Die szenischen Dichtungen der Nelly Sachs*. Frankfurt: Suhrkamp, 1966.

Schaeffer, Susan Fromberg. *Anya*. 1st ed. New York: Macmillan, 1974. 2nd ed. Avon Books, 1976 (text used).

Schneider, Gertrude. *Journey into Terror: The Story of the Riga Ghetto*. New York: Irvington, 1981.

Spritzer, Jenny. *Ich war Nr. 10291*. 2nd ed. Darmstadt: Verlag Darmstädter Blätter, 1980.

Tillion, Germaine. *Ravensbrück*. Garden City, N.Y.: Doubleday, 1975.

Trepman, Paul. *Among Men and Beasts*. Trans. Shoshana Perla and Gertrude Hirschler. South Brunswick, N.J. and New York: A.S. Barnes and Co. and Bergen-Belsen Memorial Press of the World Federation of Bergen-Belsen Associations, 1978.

Weiss, Reska. *Journey Through Hell*. London: Vallentine, Mitchell, 1961.

Wiesel, Elie. *Night; Dawn; The accident: Three tales*. New York: Hill and Wang, 1972.

Critical and Historical Literature

Alexander, Edward. *The Resonance of Dust: Essays on Holocaust Literature and Jewish Fate*. Columbus: Ohio State University Press, 1979.

Arndt, Ino. "Das Frauenkonzentrationslager Ravensbrück," in Hans Rothfels and Theodor Eschenburg, *Studien zur Geschichte der Konzentrationslager*. Stuttgart: Deutsche Verlags-Anstalt, 1970.

Bauer, Yehuda. *The Holocaust in Historical Perspective*. Seattle: University of Washington Press, 1978.

———. "Whose Holocaust?" *Midstream* (November, 1980): 42–46.

Bettelheim, Bruno. *The Informed Heart. Autonomy in a Mass Age*. Glencoe, Ill.: Free Press, 1960.

———. *Surviving and Other Essays*. New York: Alfred A. Knopf, 1979.

The Black Book: The Nazi Crime Against the Jewish People. New York: The Jewish Black Book Committee, 1946.

Bosmajian, Hamida. *Metaphors of Evil. Contemporary German Literature and the Shadow of Nazism*. Iowa City: University of Iowa Press, 1979.

Bridenthal, Renate; Grossman, Atina; and Kaplan, Marion. *When Biology Became Destiny: Women in Weimar and Nazi Germany*. New York: Monthly Review Press, 1984.

Brownmiller, Susan L. *Against Our Will: Men, Women, and Rape*. New York: Simon and Schuster, 1975.

Brozan, Nadine. "Holocaust Women: A Study in Survival," *New York Times*, March 23, 1983, pp. C–1, 16.

Chodorow, Nancy. *The Reproduction of Mothering*. Berkeley: University of California Press, 1978.

Dawidowicz, Lucy. *The War Against the Jews 1933–1945*. New York: Bantam, 1976.

Delaney, Janice; Lupton, Mary Jane; and Toth, Emily. *The Curse: A Cultural History of Menstruation*. New York: The New American Library, 1976.

Des Pres, Terrence. *The Survivor*. New York: Oxford University Press, 1976.

Ellman, Mary. *Thinking About Women*. New York: Harcourt, Brace, and World, 1968.

Ezrahi, Sidra Dekoven. *By Words Alone: The Holocaust in Literature*. Chicago: The University of Chicago Press, 1980.

Fein, Helen. *Accounting for Genocide. National Responses and Jewish Victimization During the Holocaust*. New York: The Free Press, 1979.

Feingold, Henry L. "Determining the Uniqueness of the Holocaust: The Factor of Historical Valence." *Shoah* 2, no. 2 (Spring, 1981): 10.

Foley, Barbara. "Fact, Fiction, Fascism: Testimony and Mimesis in Holocaust Narratives." *Comparative Literature* 34, no. 4 (Fall, 1982): 330–60.

Fussell, Paul. *The Great War and Modern Memory*. New York: Oxford University Press, 1975.

Grobman, Alex, and Landes, Daniel, eds. *Genocide. Critical Issues of the Holocaust*. Los Angeles: The Simon Wiesenthal Center, and Chappaqua, N.Y.: Rossel Books, 1983.

Haft, Cynthia. *The Theme of Nazi Concentration Camps in French Literature*. The Hague, Paris: Mouton, 1973.

Hilberg, Raul. *Destruction of the European Jews*. Chicago: Quadrangle Books, 1961; New York: Holmes and Meier, 1985, rev. ed.

Huyssen, Andreas. "The Politics of Identification." *New German Critique* 19 (Winter, 1980): 117–36.

Jelinek, Estelle. *Women's Autobiography*. Bloomington: Indiana University Press, 1980.

Kelly (Gadol), Joan. "The Social Relations of the Sexes: Methodological Implications of Women's History." *Signs* 1, no. 4 (Summer, 1976).

Kirkpatrick, Clifford. *Nazi Germany: Its Women and Family Life*. Indianapolis: Bobbs-Merrill Company, 1938.

Koonz, Claudia. "Nazi Women Before 1933: Rebels Against Emancipation." *Social Science Quarterly* 56 (1976): 553–63.

Lamont, Rosette C. "Charlotte Delbo's Frozen Friezes." *Esprit Créateur* 19, no. 2 (Summer, 1979): 65–74.

————. "Literature, the Exile's Agent of Survival: Alexander Solzhenitsyn and Charlotte Delbo." *Mosaic* 9, no. 1 (Fall, 1975): 1–17.

Langer, Lawrence L. *The Age of Atrocity: Death in Modern Literature.* Boston: Beacon Press, 1978.

————. *The Holocaust and the Literary Imagination.* New Haven: Yale University Press, 1975.

————. *Versions of Survival. The Holocaust and the Human Spirit.* Albany: State University of New York Press, 1982.

Millett, Kate. *Sexual Politics.* Garden City, N.Y.: Doubleday and Company, 1970.

Pawełczyńska, Anna. *Values and Violence in Auschwitz.* Berkeley and Los Angeles: University of California Press, 1979.

Rector, Frank. *The Nazi Extermination of Homosexuals.* New York: Stein and Day, 1981.

Reich, Wilhelm. *The Mass Psychology of Fascism.* Trans. Vincent Carfagno. New York: Farrar, Straus, and Giroux, 1970.

Reitlinger, Gerald. *The Final Solution: The Attempt to Exterminate the Jews of Europe, 1939–1945.* 2nd rev. and augm. ed. South Brunswick, N. J.: T. Yoseloff, 1961.

Ribalow, Harold U. *The Tie That Binds. Conversations with Jewish Writers.* San Diego: A. S. Barnes, 1980.

Ringelheim, Joan Miriam. "The Unethical and the Unspeakable: Women and the Holocaust." *Simon Wiesenthal Center Annual* 1 (1984): 79–80.

————. "Women and the Holocaust: A Reconsideration of Research." *Signs* 10, no. 4 (Summer, 1985): 741–61.

Rosenfeld, Alvin. *A Double Dying.* Bloomington: Indiana University Press, 1980.

————, and Greenberg, Irving, eds. *Confronting the Holocaust: The Impact of Elie Wiesel.* Bloomington: Indiana University Press, 1979.

Scholz-Klink, Gertrud. "Weg und Aufgabe der nationalsozialistischen Frauenbewegung." In Semmelroth, Ellen and von Stieda, Renate, *N.S. Frauenbuch.* München: J. F. Lehmanns Verlag, 1934.

Spengemann, William C. *The Forms of Autobiography: Episodes in the History of the Literary Genre.* New Haven: Yale University Press, 1980.

Stephenson, Jill. *Women in Nazi Society.* New York: Barnes and Noble-Harper and Row, 1975.

Suhl, Yuri, ed. *They Fought Back: The Story of the Jewish Resistance in Nazi Europe.* New York: Crown Publishers, 1967.

Syrkin, Marie. *Blessed Is the Match.* Philadelphia: Knopf, 1947.

INDEX

56; and loss of families, 14; not
gassed for paternity, 18; as
Oedipal objects, 111, 112;
primary parenting and male
friendship, 113; in Schaeffer, 52;
and sons in camps, 101-4; in
Wiesel, 101-2, 107, 112
Feingold, Henry, 1
Feelings, 56, 110. *See also* Inmate relations
Fénelon, Fania, 1, 32, 85, 90,
131; amenorrhea, 18-19;
authenticity, 121, 123, 125;
inmate relations, 86, 111-12;
mothers, 25-26; sexual abuse,
27, 29, 31, 33; style analysis,
43-45, 47
Fiction. *See* Genre; Novels
Film, "Seven Beauties," 32, 129
Foley, Barbara, 39
Frank, Anne, 1
Freud, Sigmund, 111
Friendship: in Borowski, 108-09;
in Fenelon, 89-91; in Goldberg,
92-93, 95; Goldberg compared
to Fenelon, 96; in Klein, 56-57;
in memoirs, 81; motive for risk,
127; in Schaeffer, 54. *See also*
Inmate relations
Fussell, Paul, 118

Gender distinctions: Aryan "chaste
maternity," 17; biological roles,
14-15; parenting, 14-15; passing
as non-Jew, 34; pre-war experiences, 14, 35, 102, 112; sexual
abuse, 16-18; universal vulnerability, 14
Genocide: Armenians, 1-2; Jews,
2, 35
Genre: distinguishing, 8-9; novels
and memoirs related, 41; and

predicting character type, 76.
See also Memoirs; Novels
German-language writers, 9-10
Ghetto: hiding in, 58; sexual
violence in, 28; Warsaw, 75
A Girl Called Judith Strick, 10,
23, 28-33, 43-46, 63-64, 68-72,
74-77, 85-86, 119, 121, 123-27,
131-32
Goldberg, Izaak, 92, 112; and
Fénelon, 96; inmate relations,
86, 91-96; physicians, 91;
pseudonym, 91; women, 3
Grese, Irma, 33

Haft, Cynthia, 14
Heimler, Eugen, 28
Help, practical and emotional,
56. *See also* Inmate relations
Herod's Children, 10, 28, 45-47,
119, 130
Herrenmoral. See Inmate relations
Hilberg, Raul, 14
Historical literature: authenticity,
117; and factual truth, 129-31;
memoirs, 6
Hitler, Adolf, 17
Holocaust: significance, 1-2;
victims, 2
Holocaust literature: function of,
2; inadequacy of language, 2;
languages of, 9; women writers
and gender issues in, 1-2, 5-6
Holocaust narratives. *See* Narra-
tives, Holocaust
Homosexuals: female, 33; male, 38
n.60. *See also* Sexual abuse
House of Dolls, 27-28, 33
Huyssen, Andreas, 130

Ich War Nummer 10291, 74-75
Imagination: in camp skits, 57;

Sterilization, 19-20, 34. *See also* Menstruation and amenorrhea

Sursis pour l'orchestre, 90, 119

Survival: and appearance, 54; and chance, 60; duration, for obedient inmates, 40; and effort, 50-51, 53; explained (self-effacing), 48-55; lack of general explanation, 55-58; narratives, 47; in resistance narratives, 61; and ties with the dead, 50, 56, 81

Survivor characters, transcendence of victimization (beating), 40, 41

Television docudramas: "Holocaust," 129-30; "Playing for Time," 1

Tell Me Another Morning, 19

This Way for the Gas, Ladies and Gentlemen, 27, 86, 108-09

The Tie That Binds, 120

Tillion, Germaine, 5-6, 84

Time, in various genres, 8

Truth, expectations in novels and memoirs, 8

Versions of Survival, 99

Warsaw Ghetto uprising, 75

Weiss, Reska, 26, 32

Wells, Leon, 9

Wertmüller, Lina, 32, 129

Wiesel, Elie, 1; females in, 3; inmate relations, 86, 100-04, 112

Women's autobiographies. *See* Autobiographies

"Women's Autobiography and the Male Tradition," 76

Women's Holocaust narratives. *See* Holocaust narratives

Women's relationships: feminist scholarship, 82; friendships, 82-83; mother-daughter, 82

Women writers: of A-bomb literature, 6; of autobiographies, 6-7

Work: and changing camp status, 74; and characterization, 39; factory, 55-57; impact on experience, 84; medical, 91-92, 97; musical, 64-67; outdoor, 43, 100, 106; privileged, 64; as punishment, 30-31; and self-esteem, 57; used for resistance, 71-72, 78

About the Author

MARLENE E. HEINEMANN is Assistant Professor of German at the University of Wyoming where she specializes in Women's Studies, Creative Writing, and Jewish Studies.